WORLD RELIGIONS
IN A
NUTSHELL

RAY COMFORT

Bridge-Logos

Alachua, Florida 32615

World Religions in a Nutshell

Published by:
Bridge-Logos
Alachua, Florida 32615, USA
www.bridgelogos.com

Printed in the United States of America

Library of Congress Control Number: 2008937529

ISBN 978-0-88270-669-6

Unless otherwise indicated, Scripture quotations are from the *New King James* version, ©1979, 1980, 1982 by Thomas Nelson Inc., Publishers, Nashville, Tennessee.

Edited by Lynn Copeland

Cover, page design, and production by Genesis Group (www.genesis-group.net)

Photos by Carol Scott, Covina, CA (www.cj-studio.com)

CONTENTS

INTRODUCTION

You are on CNN, live. The host leans across to you and asks, "What's the difference between Christianity and the other major religions? They are basically all the same, aren't they?" Millions are awaiting your reply. Do you know how you would answer that? Most of us are not as prepared as we should be, for this all-important task.

Sadly, most of the contemporary Church falls way short of the Book of Acts. Every page I turn in the book, I find that at every corner they turned, they preached Christ crucified. They knew their agenda and nothing was going to stop them.

Nowadays statistics tell us that 95% of the Church rarely share the gospel, even in the face of the Great Commission. The fact that we have had to be commanded to preach the gospel of everlasting life reveals something about our character. Imagine a doctor, who holds a cure to cancer in his hand, having to be *told* to give the cure to his dying patients. Imagine if he complained, "I don't know what to say," or "What if they reject me?" or "It's not my gifting." What would that tell you about his character?

Yet such is the average contemporary Christian. God has granted *everlasting life* through the gospel to a dying world, and we hesitate because we don't know what to say or because we fear rejection, etc. What does that say about our character? Spurgeon said that we should be ashamed at the "mere suspicion of unconcern."

I'm grateful that you picked up this book because you want to learn about other religions. Perhaps you want to gain knowledge because you enjoy debating with people of other faiths. Keep in mind that, while the fisher of men will occasionally get into a debate, our ultimate goal should be to persuade the lost that they need a Savior. That takes more than a knowledge of what they believe. There is something else that is necessary. It's the ability (with God's help) to show that Christianity offers something utterly unique among world religions. It provides the solution that "works righteousness" religions do not and cannot provide—complete and utter forgiveness of sins.

I don't mind admitting to you that books on world religions, with a spine the size of my fist, intimidate me. While they might look impressive on my shelf, I literally have little time for them. I want a book that will say "Here's what you need; now go to battle"—a book that will give me what I need in a nutshell.

I hope that this publication does that for you.

JUDAISM

There are approximately 14 million Jewish people in the world today, with close to 6 million living in the U.S. and about 5 million in Israel. Although Christians believe in the God of Abraham, Isaac, and Jacob and are followers of the Jewish Messiah, we don't have as much in common with our Jewish friends as you may think.

Judaism is ranked as the sixth largest organized religion in the world, but it may surprise you to find that many Jewish people don't believe in God. It's amazing, but it's true. More than half of all Jews in Israel today call themselves "secular," and according to a recent poll, only 30% of all Jews are "absolutely certain" that God exists, 34% are "somewhat certain," 24% aren't sure, and 12% believe there is no God.[1]

So it's possible to be secular, agnostic, and *even an atheist* and still be Jewish. Some Jews even believe in reincarnation. If your mother is Jewish, that makes you Jewish, no matter what you believe. So being Jewish is not the same thing as following the religion of Judaism. Being Jewish is like having a *citizenship*; but following Judaism is living a certain lifestyle. To Jewish people, what they believe about God and the afterlife isn't as important as how they live.

Background

There are three main branches, or movements, in contemporary Judaism:

Orthodox: Orthodox is the most strict form, and until 200 years ago, it was the *only* kind of Judaism. Orthodox or "traditional" Jews emphasize tradition and pride themselves on faithfully keeping the Laws of Moses. They make up 10% of the Jewish population in America.

Reform: On the other end of the scale is the liberal or "modern" movement, called Reform. The Reform movement began in the 18th century to bring Judaism's "old and outmoded ways of thinking" up to date. Reform Jews say they keep the good values of Judaism, but don't have to keep strict religious laws. These are most of the Jews you'll meet today.

Conservative: In between the Orthodox and Reform are the Conservatives. Conservative Judaism arose in the 19th century, as a middle ground between the other two branches. They're traditional but believe the rabbis can change Jewish laws to suit the times. About 30% of American Jews are Conservative.

Because Judaism emphasizes behavior instead of theology, there is a wide variety of beliefs even within each of the branches. With such diversity, it's difficult to generalize about their beliefs.

Who is God?

Orthodox Jews believe there is only one God. He is a Spirit who is all-knowing, all-powerful, ever-present, and eternal. Jews often recite something called the *Shema:*

> "Hear, O Israel: The LORD our God, the LORD is one!"
> (Deuteronomy 6:4)

Reform Jews, however, can interpret the "God concept" however they like, and that's still within the boundaries of their Judaism. They can be atheists, naturalists, religious humanists, but they all agree on one concept: "The truth is that we do not know the truth." So if you want to know what Reform Jews believe about God today, it really depends on which Jewish person you ask.

Scriptures

Orthodox Jews (the strict believers) believe that the Torah was written by God through the hand of Moses. The Torah is the Hebrew name for the first five books of the Bible: Genesis, Exodus, Leviticus, Numbers, and Deuteronomy. They also believe the rest of the Old Testament, which is called the Tanakh, but don't give it as much authority as the Torah. There is also the Talmud—the teachings of the Jewish rabbis—which they believe has great authority.

But Reform Jews (the more liberal ones) don't necessarily believe that the Scriptures were written by God. Most believe they were merely written by men. They feel it's a good book for preserving history and culture, and helps to live a good life, but the bottom line is, it wasn't written by God, so it's not binding.

Heaven and Hell

Orthodox Jews do believe there is life after death in the *Olam Ha-Ba*—the World to Come. They believe that the righteous of all nations will live forever with God in a perfect place of peace and prosperity, and that the unrighteous will suffer—but they don't all agree on where those people will go. Some believe nothing happens when you die. Others believe you go to She'ol, or Gehenna, a place of purification (kind of like a Jewish purgatory). Then you either go directly to Paradise, or you are destroyed and cease to exist, or you continue to live in a state of unending remorse. Again, today's Judaism leaves it open to personal opinion.

In the Reform and Conservative branches, most have no concept of personal life after death. What is most important is the here and now—being a good person, and making the world a better place.

Sin and Salvation

None of the branches of Judaism believe in original sin. They teach that man is created in the image of God and is born morally pure. They either think of humanity as neutral—with the potential for both good and bad—or as basically good. Although men do sin, they believe that God's justice is tempered with mercy.

Many Jewish people never ask the question, "What do I have to do to get into Heaven?" since Judaism teaches that all good people from all nations will go to Heaven. And because most Jews don't believe in Hell, they don't think of needing to be "saved" from anything. Remember, they believe they already have a favored standing with God as His "chosen people."

Many Jews do believe that studying the Torah, praying, and doing good deeds will earn them a *better* place in Heaven, but they get a "Free Pass" as descendants of Abraham, Isaac, and Jacob. Scripture has something to say about that kind of thinking:

> "And do not think to say to yourselves, 'We have Abraham as our father.' For I say to you that God is able to raise up children to Abraham from these stones." (Matthew 3:9)

The Messiah

So, what do Jewish people think about the Messiah today? Again, it depends on who you ask. Most Jewish people aren't waiting with anticipation for a coming Messiah. The Orthodox Jews are still holding to that hope, but they fail to see the Messiah as divine, or as having to suffer as the Scriptures prophesied that He would. They believe that the Messiah is simply going to be a great political leader who brings peace to Israel and extends his rule over all the earth. One thing most Jewish people do agree on today is that Jesus is not that Messiah.

The other branches place their hope not in a person but in a "messianic age"—a Utopian age that mankind is progressing toward.

Jewish Customs

It is traditional for most Jews to celebrate certain life events, such as circumcision of male newborns, and a *bar mitzvah* (for boys) or *bat mitzvah* (for girls)—which is a coming-of-age ceremony at age 13. Many also observe the Sabbath as a weekly day of rest.

Most Jewish people observe at least some of the Jewish holidays, though it's often to connect with their heritage more than for religious reasons. The most solemn are the High Holy Days: Rosh Hashanah and Yom Kippur. Yom Kippur, the Day of Atonement, is when Jews fast and pray for the forgiveness of their sins.

The most popular of all the holidays is Passover, which remembers the Israelites' deliverance from slavery in Egypt. During the week of Passover they eat *matzo*, which is unleavened bread, and hold a *Seder*, or Passover meal.

How to Reach a Jewish Person

First, here are some tips on what *not* to do as you're talking with a Jewish person:

- Don't be intimidated by thinking that all Jewish people are well acquainted with the Scriptures. Although they do give the Old Testament respect, there's a very good chance you know the Bible better than they do.

- Unless it's in a phrase like "Orthodox Jews," using the word "Jews" can sound anti-Semitic. It's best to refer to "Jewish people" instead.

- Since they view Jewishness as a way of life, avoid using the term "convert," which implies leaving behind their Jewishness. Instead, talk about becoming a "follower of Jesus."

- While it's fine to mention "Y'shua" as the Hebrew name of Jesus, people will not realize that you are referring to the historical person Jesus of Nazareth unless you also use the name "Jesus."

- The term "Savior" is not understood by Jewish people, so instead speak of a Redeemer and use the word "Messiah." Because of the Passover *Seder*, the concept of "redemption" is more familiar, so use that term rather than "salvation." You can explain that as God freed the Israelites from slavery in Egypt, so He wants to free us from the slavery to sin in our lives.

It shouldn't surprise us that Jewish people are difficult to reach with the gospel. One reason is that many of them equate Christianity with Roman Catholicism. And why shouldn't they? When they watch the news at Christmas or Easter, who is upheld as "the head of the Christian Church"? The pope. They therefore believe that Christians bow down to graven images and that they worship Mary and many other saints. To them, Christianity is a false religion, and should be kept at arm's length because it directly violates the First and Second Commandments.

Many Jews even equate Christianity with Adolf Hitler —despite the fact that biblical Christianity is soaked in love of humanity, while Hitler's philosophy was saturated in the blood of pure hatred. Hitler infiltrated the church by installing his own leaders and Nazi "pastors," then used the church structure to mock the Bible and teach that Jews were "children of the devil." So in the eyes of many Jews, the evil of Nazism came directly through the Christian church.

As a result, when we approach Jewish people with a New Testament in our hand, or a cross around our neck and sweetly say, "I would like to talk to you about Jesus," to them we might as well be saying, "Hi, I represent an institution that is filled with pedophiles, bows down to idols, worships false gods, and was responsible for the murder of six million Jews." No wonder they are reluctant to talk with us.

So, how do we reach a Jewish person? Well, there are many different ways you could try. Paul said he reasoned with the Jews both out of the Law of Moses and out of the Prophets, so you could show them how Jesus fulfills the Jewish prophecies of the coming Messiah. (For just a few of the many fulfilled prophecies, see the "Messianic Prophecies" chart on the following page.) But sadly, many Jews don't care about this evidence because they don't have much regard for the Scriptures. And, if you have someone who esteems the Old Testament, he may argue that you're just "reading Jesus into the Scriptures."

MESSIANIC PROPHECIES

PROPHECY	FULFILLMENT
Messiah will be from the lineage of Abraham (Gen. 18:18); Isaac (Gen. 21:12); Jacob (Gen. 28:13,14); Judah (Gen. 49:10); Jesse (Isa. 11:1,2,10); and David (Jer. 23:5,6).	"Jesus...the son of David, the son of Jesse,...the son of Judah, the son of Jacob, the son of Isaac, the son of Abraham." (Luke 3:31–34)
Messiah will be born of a virgin. (Isaiah 7:14)	"An angel of the Lord appeared to him in a dream, saying, 'Joseph, son of David, do not be afraid to take to you Mary your wife, for that which is conceived in her is of the Holy Spirit. And she will bring forth a Son, and you shall call His name JESUS, for He will save His people from their sins.'" (Matt. 1:20,21)
Messiah will be born in Bethlehem. (Micah 5:2)	"Now after Jesus was born in Bethlehem of Judea in the days of Herod the king, behold, wise men from the East came to Jerusalem, saying, 'Where is He who has been born King of the Jews?'" (Matt. 2:1,2)
Messiah will be declared the Son of God. (Psalm 2:7)	"Suddenly a voice came from heaven, saying, 'This is My beloved Son, in whom I am well pleased.'" (Matt. 3:17)
Messiah will perform miraculous healings. (Isaiah 35:5,6)	"Jesus answered and said to them, 'Go and tell John the things you have seen and heard: that the blind see, the lame walk, the lepers are cleansed, the deaf hear, the dead are

MESSIANIC PROPHECIES (CONT'D)

PROPHECY	FULFILLMENT
	raised, the poor have the gospel preached to them.'" (Luke 7:21,22)
Messiah will be betrayed for thirty pieces of silver. (Zechariah 11:12)	"Then one of the twelve, called Judas Iscariot, went to the chief priests and said, 'What are you willing to give me if I deliver Him to you?' And they counted out to him thirty pieces of silver." (Matt. 26:14,15)
Messiah will be crucified. (Psalm 22:16)	"And He, bearing His cross, went out to a place called…Golgotha, where they crucified Him, and two others with Him, one on either side, and Jesus in the center." (John 19:17,18)
Messiah will not have any bones broken. (Psalm 34:20)	"Then the soldiers came and broke the legs of the first and of the other who was crucified with Him. But when they came to Jesus and saw that He was already dead, they did not break His legs." (John 19:32,33)
Messiah will be resurrected. (Psalm 16:10)	"[David], foreseeing this, spoke concerning the resurrection of the Christ, that His soul was not left in Hades, nor did His flesh see corruption. This Jesus God has raised up, of which we are all witnesses." (Acts 2:31,32)
Messiah will ascend to heaven. (Psalm 16:10)	"So then, after the Lord had spoken to them, He was received up into heaven, and sat down at the right hand of God." (Mark 16:19)

Another approach is to try to answer all of the person's objections to Christianity. For example, how we as Christians can believe in the Trinity and yet believe in only one God, not three, or that Jesus will set up His earthly kingdom at His *second* coming, not His first. All this information is good, but be forewarned: if you are speaking to someone who has a proud heart, this may stir up a zesty argument.

That's why when we talk with a Jewish person about God, we must start with the Law of Moses. It's really very simple, so don't complicate it. Find out if the person is proud or humble by asking the question, "Would you consider yourself to be a good person?" If he says "yes," then take him through the Ten Commandments, just like Jesus did with the rich young ruler (see Mark 10:17). Let those ten great cannons humble him and show him that he'll be guilty on Judgment Day and will need God's forgiveness, which can be found only in the Messiah, Jesus Christ.

If his heart is humble, then unashamedly reveal the love of God displayed on the cross—that God Himself provided a Lamb for our atonement. Then trust in His great faithfulness to bring the person to everlasting life that is in Jesus alone.

Witnessing to a Jewish Person

You: Hello. Nice day.[2]

Jeremiah: Yes, it is.

You: Where are you from?

Jeremiah: New York.

You: I love New York. Amazing place. My name is Ray.

Jeremiah: I'm Jeremiah.

You: Nice to meet you, Jeremiah

Jeremiah: Nice to meet you, too.

You: I have a question for you, Jeremiah. What do you think happens after someone dies? Do you think there's a Heaven? Do people get reincarnated?

Jeremiah: I don't know.

You: Do you think about it?

Jeremiah: Sometimes. I'm Jewish.

[You need not panic and begin trying to prove that Jesus was the promised Messiah. Your aim at this point is simply to bring the knowledge of sin, using the Law, so that he will see that he needs God's mercy.]

You: So you think Heaven exists?

Jeremiah: I hope so.

[A statement like this should put you at ease. Jeremiah is human. He *thinks* about the issues of life and death. His "I hope so" reveals that he's not angry or anti-God.]

You: Do you think that you are good enough to go there?

Jeremiah: Yes, I believe so. [See Proverbs 20:6.]

You: Have you kept the Law of Moses?

[The reason a Jew thinks that he is a good person is found in Romans 10:3. It says of the Jews, "For they being ignorant of God's righteousness, and seeking to establish their own right-eousness, have not submitted to the righteousness of God." The opening of the spiritual nature of the Law will show him God's standard of righteousness. Jews have the Law of Moses, but like the Pharisees they twist it or ignore it, therefore making it void to themselves.]

Jeremiah: Sort of.

[If he says that he has broken the Commandments, ask which ones. Then still go through the Law. You need to *personalize* his sin, as Paul did in Romans 2:21–24.]

You: Let's go through a few of the Commandments to see how you do. How many lies do you think you have told, in your whole life? I don't mean "white" lies—*real* lies.

[You will regret it if you don't make a distinction between what he perceives as permissible lies and "deceitfulness." He will more than likely trivialize his lying, if you don't get an admission from him that he has actually borne false witness.]

Jeremiah: Lots.

You: Lots? Five? Ten? Hundreds?

Jeremiah: Hundreds?

[People will often boast of their lies, because at this point there's no accountability to God. So they are more than happy to admit their sins.]

You: What do you call someone who tells lies?

Jeremiah: Human.

You: Yes. But what would you call *me* if I told lies?

Jeremiah: A liar.

You: We often think lightly of lying, calling them "fibs" or "white lies," yet Scripture tells us that "lying lips are an abomination to the Lord." That means lies are "extremely detestable" to Him. Have you ever stolen anything, in your whole life?

Jeremiah: Yes. I have, in the past, when I was younger.

[It is normal for people to trivialize sin with phrases such as, "Just little things," "When I was young," etc.]

You: What do you call someone who steals things?

Jeremiah: A thief.

You: Have you ever used God's name in vain?

Jeremiah: Plenty of times. I know it's wrong.

[Don't hesitate to gently show the serious nature of sin. This is extremely important. If he thinks lightly of his sins, then he won't see the mercy of God in offering forgiveness. The greater he sees his transgressions, the greater he will understand God's love expressed at the cross.]

You: Think about that. God gave you life. He gave you eyes to see the beauty of this creation. He gave you ears to enjoy good music, taste buds to enjoy good food. He lavished His goodness upon you, and then you used His holy name as a cuss word to express disgust. That's a very serious sin—one that is called "blasphemy."

Jeremiah: I know it's bad.

[It is a great encouragement when someone admits their sins like this.]

You: Jesus said, "Whoever looks at a woman to lust for her has already committed adultery with her in his heart." Have you ever done that?

[If you are anything like me, you will be concerned that you will turn a Jewish person off if you quote Jesus. But whatever you do, don't hesitate to say "Jesus said." Remember that Jesus *was* a Jew (see John 4:9) and that the first 8,000 Christians in the Book of Acts were Jewish. Always remember, when you are using this verse you are quoting the Word of God, which is living and powerful (see Hebrews 4:12).]

Jeremiah: Plenty of times.

You: Then you have committed adultery in God's eyes. So, Jeremiah, here's a summation of what we have found. You are not a "good" person. By your own admission (I'm not judging you), you are a lying, thieving, blasphemous, adulterer at heart.

Jeremiah: Wow. I never thought of it like that . . .

You: And you have to face God on Judgment Day. If He judges you by the Ten Commandments, will you be innocent or guilty?

Jeremiah: I will be guilty.

You: Will you go to Heaven or Hell?

Jeremiah: I think I will still go to Heaven.

You: Why?

Jeremiah: Because those things were in the past. Besides, I'm Jewish. We are the chosen people.

You: Being Jewish doesn't mean that you get an automatic pass. So, when did you last lust after a woman?

Jeremiah: A few minutes ago. Okay, I see what you are saying, but *most* bad things I've done were a long time ago.

You: Actually, *everything* you have done has been "in the past," and God sees the sins of your youth as though it were yesterday. If you died today, you have God's promise that you won't go to Heaven. The Bible warns that all liars will have their part in the lake of fire. No thief, no blasphemer or adulterer will inherit the Kingdom of God. Does it concern you that if you died right now, you would go to Hell, forever?

Jeremiah: Yes, it does.

You: That makes sense. You love life. Do you know what God did for us, so that we could avoid Hell?

Jeremiah: No. What did He do?

You: Do you remember what happened at Passover?

Jeremiah: Yes.

You: Moses instructed the children of Israel to put the blood of the lamb on the door posts, so that death would "pass over" them. All those who applied the blood were saved from death. When John the Baptist saw Jesus for the first time, he said, "Behold, the Lamb of God who takes away the sin of the world!" This is clearly spoken of in Isaiah 53. God became a Man in Jesus of Nazareth. The Bible says that God "was manifest in the flesh," and the reason for that was so that as "the lamb of God" His blood could cause death to pass over us. He came to suffer and die for the sin of the world.

We broke His Law (the Ten Commandments) but because Jesus paid our fine on the cross 2,000 years ago, God can forgive us. God can dismiss your case. He can commute your death sentence. The Bible says, "God demonstrates His own love toward us, in that while we were still sinners, Christ died for us." God proved His great love for you through the cross. Then Jesus rose from the dead, and defeated the power of the grave. If you repent and trust the Savior, God will forgive your sins and grant you everlasting life. What you need to do is repent and trust the Savior that God provided. Does that make sense?

Jeremiah: Yes, it does.

You: Jeremiah, you aren't guaranteed tomorrow. That comes only by the grace of God. So if you died today, where would you go?

Jeremiah: I would probably go to Hell.

You: So what are you going to do about it?

Jeremiah: I need to pray.

You: That's right. Repent and trust the Savior. When are you going to do that?

Jeremiah: Right now.

You: Thanks for listening to me.

Jeremiah: Thank *you.*

From Judaism to Christ

Years ago, my wife made a comment that our marriage could only be better if we invited God in. In my pride and desire to live with the personal religion I'd created, I said, "Oh, really? Which God—yours or mine? You believe in some guy who died 2,000 years ago and I believe in God. Are you planning on going to a synagogue? Because there's no way I'm going into a Catholic church." Result: Discussion over.

After moving to Georgia, good friends of ours (who were Christians) consistently showed us love and kindness and were more than willing to answer my ignorant questions about what Christians believed. I learned that true believers in Christ (which I found was the Greek word for *Messiah*) would never believe in Replacement Theology nor would they have done acts like the pogroms or the Holocaust. True believers in the Messiah of Israel would only show their love for Israel and their love for the Messiah's people, the Jews. They were faithful to answer my questions and go no further. They must have known that my pride would have pushed me the other way.

These friends asked my wife to go to church with them and I had no problem with her going—I'd assumed that there would be no change in our lives. The day my wife came home and shared with me that she'd become a "born-again Christian" immediately brought me back to a day 20 years prior: My brother came home from college and shared that his best friend had become a "born-again Christian." I'd never heard the term before. It would be another 20 years before I heard it again. My father's response had stuck with me so subconsciously that I couldn't believe it came back so quickly and so clearly: "Those are the worst kind," he said. This was exactly what popped into my head when my wife told me of her decision.

Life slowly started changing. My pride reared its ugly head once again as I heard her teach our two-year-old daughter how to thank Jesus for our food: "What are you doing thanking a dead guy for the food I worked for?" When it came to the small fish symbol on the back of her car: "Do you realize people will think that I believe in *your* Jesus when I'm in your car?"

I concluded that I had to stop this. I spoke with an Orthodox Jew who was close to both my wife and me. Her response was disheartening: "I'll tell you, there are only two possibilities in a mixed marriage like yours—divorce or conversion." I didn't talk with her again about it. I spoke with a rabbi, but his response was lacking. I knew I couldn't speak with a Gentile believer because he wouldn't have the Jewish perspective that I needed; besides, his mind would be already made up. I'd have to look for myself into the Book I never wanted to look into before—the Hebrew Scriptures.

After a year of studying and seeing irrefutable evidence in prophecy and seeing that there are no contradictions in Scripture, I realized the amazing fingerprint of God throughout this Book. Days before Passover, a Jewish believer in Jesus was speaking on "Messiah in the Passover" at my wife's church. After seeing his presentation, I spoke with his wife and she asked, "So, what do you do with Isaiah 53?" I asked what she was talking about. We grabbed a Bible and she had me read it. It was the straw that broke the camel's back, but my pride wouldn't relinquish its grip just yet.

I stewed on this for another couple of days. Then the day before Passover, I humbled myself in order to ask the Lord to forgive me and to cover me with His blood as He did the doorposts in Egypt. Where my wife felt overwhelming peace in receiving His Gift, I wept. I was overcome with the realization that He died for my transgressions as so clearly stated in Isaiah 53.

—Scott D.

MORMONISM

M any of us don't really know much about the Mormons. We know that their missionaries wear white shirts, ride bikes, and go around two-by-two. We also know that they have an intense interest in genealogies, and air family-oriented TV commercials in which they offer a free Bible and a Book of Mormon. In fact, they spent more than $100 million in advertising in the 1990s.

There are currently over 13 million Mormons worldwide in 176 nations, with about 6 million members in the U.S. Due to their advertising and missionary efforts, they claim to be "one of the fastest growing Christian faiths in the world." Using words like "repent," "salvation," "gospel," and "grace," they certainly *sound* Christian. But do their beliefs line up with the Bible?

Background

Many years ago, a 14-year-old boy named Joseph Smith, Jr., said he had a vision while he was praying in the woods. He claimed he was visited by God the Father and Jesus, who told him that Christianity had become corrupt. They said that all the existing churches were wrong, their creeds were an abomination, and he shouldn't join any of them.

Three years later Smith said he was visited by an angel named Moroni, who told him where to find some buried golden plates that would explain the true gospel. Smith supposedly was able to miraculously translate these plates from "Reformed Egyptian" into English, and the result eventually became known as the *Book of Mormon: Another Testament of Jesus Christ.*

Mormonism began in Palmyra, New York, in the 1820s. Joseph Smith said that God chose him to restore the true church in North America, and he officially launched the Church of Jesus Christ of Latter-day Saints. Though they're commonly known as "Mormons," church members prefer to be called "Latter-day Saints."

Scriptures

Latter-day Saints formulate their beliefs from five main sources:

1) The Book of Mormon, which Joseph Smith said is "the most correct of any book on earth"

2) *The Doctrine and Covenants* (which is mostly about theology)

3) *The Pearl of Great Price*

4) The King James Bible, "insofar as it is translated correctly"—for the average Mormon this means that the Bible cannot be trusted, which is why Joseph Smith began his own "inspired" translation.

5) The ultimate authority that tops them all is the living Mormon apostles and prophets, especially the Mormon church president, considered to be the final authority and voice of God on earth today—kind of like a Mormon pope. What he says goes. And he can overturn any teaching of a previous president—which they often do.

Let's look at what they believe about God.

Who is God?

Joseph Smith's "new revelation" is really the oldest lie in the Book: that man can become like God. The Mormons' main belief can be summed up in what they call the law of eternal progression:

> "As man is, God once was. As God is, man may become." (Mormon prophet Lorenzo Snow, 5th LDS President)

The Mormon church teaches that "Heavenly Father" is not eternal but is a created being with a body of flesh and bones just like ours. He began as a mortal man on another planet and, through learning and obedience, progressed to become a god and was given this planet to rule. He was originally no different than we are.

"God himself was once as we are now, and is an exalted man, and sits enthroned in yonder heavens!!! ... We have imagined that God was God from all eternity. I will refute that idea and take away the veil, so that you may see." (*Teachings of the Prophet Joseph Smith*, p. 345)

Today, he lives on a planet that circles a star named Kolob (*Pearl of Great* Price, pp. 34-35). The Mormon God, known as Elohim, is also married and has many wives. According to Mormon teaching, there are literally millions of gods ruling millions of planets, and Mormons believe that they too can become a god like him and be given their own planet to rule over.

In essence, Mormon teaching humanizes God and deifies man.

The Bible, however, says that God is *always* the same, He never changes, and there is no other God anywhere besides Him (other "gods" are false gods):

- "I am the LORD, I do not change." (Malachi 3:6)

- "Thus says the LORD... I am the First and I am the Last; besides Me there is no God." (Isaiah 44:6)

- "You are My witnesses, says the LORD...Before Me there was no God formed, nor shall there be after Me." (Isaiah 43:10)

- "I am God, and there is no other; I am God, and there is none like Me." (Isaiah 46:9)

Who is Jesus?

The Latter-day Saints teach that all people pre-existed in the spiritual realm before they were born physically. When God came to this planet he brought his goddess wives, and they began producing spirit children who grew and matured in the spirit realm. Jesus (known then as Jehovah) was the first of their spirit children to be born in Heaven, followed by Lucifer, and then the rest of us.

> "In the pre-mortal spirit life, Jesus, Lucifer, and all of us were the spirit children of God and His wives." (*Journal of Discourses*, Vol. XI, p. 122)

So Mormons believe that Jesus and Satan are spirit brothers and that we were all born as their siblings in Heaven. Jesus is considered to be the "only begotten Son" because Heavenly Father himself came down to earth and had sexual relations with Mary to produce the body of Jesus. This is disputed among many Mormons and not always "officially" taught and believed. Nevertheless, Brigham Young, the 2nd prophet of the Mormon church, taught it (*Journal of Discourses*, Vol. 4, p. 218). Mormons also teach that Jesus was married to multiple wives and had children.

Therefore, in Mormon theology, Jesus is not God incarnate, the eternal Creator, who was begotten by the Holy Spirit. Mormons deny the Trinity and believe that Heavenly Father, Jesus Christ, and the Holy Ghost are three separate gods.

Therefore, instead of teaching that Jesus is our immortal God who became a man, the LDS church teaches that Jesus is a mortal man who *became* a god and showed that all men can do the same. That certainly isn't the Jesus of the Bible.

The Scriptures warn against preaching "another Jesus" (2 Cor. 11:4) and that Satan himself can appear to us as an "angel of light." Joseph Smith said it was an "angel" clothed in light that gave him "another testament"—which has another "gospel" entirely. According to the Bible, it is absolutely crucial that we have the true Jesus and the true gospel. Listen to these stinging words of warning from the apostle Paul:

> I marvel that you are turning away so soon from Him who called you in the grace of Christ, to a *different gospel*, which is not another; but there are some who trouble you and want to pervert the gospel of Christ. But even if we, or *an angel from heaven*, preach any other gospel to you than what we have preached to you, let him be accursed. As we have said before, so now I say again, if anyone preaches any other gospel to you than what you have received, let him be accursed. (Galatians 1:6–9, emphasis added)

Heaven and Hell

Mormons believe that, after the final judgment, almost everyone will go to some form of Heaven. There are three levels of Heaven: celestial, terrestrial, and telestial. All of them are superior to this life. Mormons seek to go to the top level, where they return to Heavenly Father and become a god of their own planet and produce lots of spirit children.

- **Celestial kingdom:** This is where Heavenly Father and Jesus Christ reside. Only faithful Mormons who meet all the requirements will enter this highest kingdom. If they live according to the gospel of Jesus Christ and are cleansed from sin by the Atonement, they will receive a place in the celestial kingdom, where they will live in God's presence and know complete joy. This celestial kingdom also has three levels with different privileges and powers.

- **Terrestrial kingdom:** Righteous people who are not Mormons—those who refuse to accept the gospel of Jesus Christ but who live honorable lives—will receive a place in the terrestrial kingdom. Most Mormons will also end up here.

- **Telestial kingdom:** The lowest level is for the wicked and ungodly—liars, thieves, adulterers, murderers, etc. Those who continue in their sins and do not repent until after they have died will eventually receive a place in the telestial kingdom. They won't be with God and Christ, but nonetheless the glory of the telestial kingdom "surpasses all understanding" (*D&C*, 76:81–90).

Mormon apostle John Widtsoe insisted there was no Hell when he said, "In the Church of Jesus Christ of Latter-day Saints, there is no hell. All will find a measure of salvation; all must pay for any infringement of the law; but the payment will be as the Lord may decide" (Joseph Smith, *Seeker After Truth*, p. 178). However, 10th LDS President Joseph Fielding Smith wrote, "The Church does teach that there is a place called hell. Of course we do not believe that all those who do not receive the gospel will eventually be cast into hell" (*Answers to Gospel Questions*, 2:210).

Mormons call the place of punishment "outer darkness," but they're taught that it's only for the "sons of perdition": the devil and his angels, and a few apostate Mormons. Even Hitler might qualify for the low level of Heaven, which Joseph Smith said is so wonderful that if we could get one little glimpse into the lowest Heaven, "we would be tempted to commit suicide to get there."

The *Doctrine and Covenants* explains what awaits Mormons who make it to the celestial kingdom:

> "Then they shall be gods, because they have no end;
> therefore shall they be from everlasting to everlasting
> … Then they shall be gods because they have all power,
> and the angels are subject to them." (132:20)

So the Mormons view Heaven not as a place where they can worship a holy God and enjoy His presence throughout all eternity. Instead, their goal is man-centered rather than God-centered. They worship the creature rather than the Creator, who alone is worthy of all praise.

Sin and Salvation

Mormons claim they believe in salvation by grace through faith in Jesus Christ, but they mean something entirely different from what the Bible teaches.

In Mormon theology, Jesus atoned for the effects of Adam's sin, allowing all mankind—good *and* bad—to be resurrected and become immortal. Everyone will therefore achieve "general salvation," and will then have the opportunity to become gods. That's why they can agree that Jesus is their "Savior." They believe He "saved" them from physical death.

> "The atonement of Jesus Christ enables God's children to overcome the effects of the Fall and to obtain eternal life by obedience." (mormon.org)

> "The first effect [of the atonement] is to secure to all mankind alike, exemption from the penalty of the fall, thus providing a plan of *General Salvation*. The second effect is to open a way for *Individual Salvation* whereby mankind may secure remission of personal sins." (James Talmage, *Articles of Faith*, pp. 78–79)

Being exalted to godhood is what they call "eternal life." To obtain "individual" or "full salvation," Mormons must meet the conditions set by the church:

- Have faith in Jesus, accept Joseph Smith and his successors as "God's mouthpiece," repent, be baptized, be a member of the LDS church.

"If it had not been for Joseph Smith and the restoration, there would be no salvation. There is no salvation outside the Church of Jesus Christ of Latter-day Saints." (Bruce McConkie, *Mormon Doctrine*, p. 670)

- Keep the Commandments, follow *all* the laws and ordinances of the church, do good works, tithe to the church.

- Keep the "Word of Wisdom" by abstaining from alcohol, tobacco, and caffeine, and be found worthy.

- *Then* they can earn a "temple recommend," which is the only way they can enter a Mormon temple. There they need to fulfill their temple work: have a Celestial Marriage, do genealogical work, be baptized for the dead, go through a set of rituals, and learn secret handshakes to enable them to enter the third level of the celestial kingdom. For those who achieve this highest of heavens, exaltation awaits them. They can become a god!

This lifelong labor to earn salvation is the new "gospel" that the "angels" gave to Joseph Smith—a salvation by works and not by faith alone. The Book of Mormon says, "For we know that it is by grace that we are saved, *after all we can do*" (2 Nephi 25:23).

Yet the Bible makes it very clear that salvation has nothing to do with our works: "For by grace you have been saved through faith, and that not of yourselves; it is the gift of God, *not of works*, lest anyone should boast" (Ephesians 2:8,9). Titus wrote, "*Not by works of righteousness which we have done,* but according to His mercy He saved us" (Titus 3:5). Salvation is a gift from God that we must receive by faith alone, because you cannot possibly do anything to earn it. But look at this quote by a Mormon prophet and church president:

> "One of the most fallacious doctrines originated by Satan and propounded by man is that man is saved alone by the grace of God; that belief in Jesus Christ alone is all that is needed for salvation." (Spencer W. Kimball, *Miracle of Forgiveness,* p. 206)

Mormon Customs

Mormons are well-known for their interest in genealogy. But do you know why? LDS members believe it is their responsibility to be baptized on behalf of the dead. If family members (or anyone) have died without accepting Mormonism, they can still make it to Heaven, if their names are taken to the Temple and someone is baptized on their behalf. Because they don't have a body, the ordinance is done for them by proxy, giving the dead the opportunity to accept Mormonism in the spirit world.

They base the practice on 1 Corinthians 15:29: "Otherwise, what will they do who are baptized for the dead, if the dead do not rise at all? Why then are they baptized for the dead?" But notice how Paul disassociates himself from the pagan practice by using the word "they," not "we."

Some Mormons are even married on behalf of the dead, by going through the marriage ceremony in their place.

This supposedly enables a dead person to make it out of "Spirit Prison" and into a higher level of Heaven.

The Mormon church has over 50,000 volunteer missionaries working throughout the world, performing community service and sharing the "gospel" of the LDS church. Missionaries are usually 19 to 21 years old, and serve for either 18 months or 2 years.

How to Reach a Mormon

We've just scratched the surface of Mormonism, but it should be very clear to you that even though Mormons use language that sounds Christian, it is not a Christian religion. It is a manmade religion invented by Joseph Smith, and it is heresy. A religion cannot teach that Jesus is the brother of Lucifer, that you and I can become gods, and that we're saved by grace "after all we can do," and still be labeled part of Christianity.

It is our responsibility to reach out to Mormons with the truth and love. If we care about them, we need to tell them there is a very real Hell and that the only way to be saved is not through the Church of Joseph Smith, but by God's grace alone, through faith in Christ alone. So how do we do that?

There are several approaches you can take. If you have a good memory and a sharp mind, you can sword fight with Mormons using some of the information we've covered. Show them who God and Jesus really are according to the Bible, and how the Mormon "gospel" is "another gospel."

But be prepared. If you get into an argument about Joseph Smith, becoming a god, and Jesus being the brother of Satan, it can get heated pretty quickly, because you're attacking the very things they—and more than likely their family and friends—believe.

There is another way to reach Mormons that is very simple and effective. Although Mormons may appear confident and self-assured on the outside, many are dealing with a great deal of stress because they are striving for perfection. That's the goal of their religion: to "be perfect as their Father in Heaven is perfect." They are taught that the only way God will bring them to Heaven is if they are "worthy." Well, the obvious question in every Mormon's mind is, "Am I worthy enough?"

What you can do is reinforce their predicament. Show them that they are not even close to being perfect or "worthy" through their efforts. The Bible says that even our good works are like filthy rags in the eyes of a holy God (Isaiah 64:6). Mormons are just like the rest of us—sinners, by nature children of wrath, separated from God because of our sins, and deserving of His terrible justice. No amount of good works can ever make anyone "perfect" or save them from eternal Hell.

You must show them that the leap they're trying to make to Heaven is a thousand times wider than the Grand Canyon—it's impossible. This is actually good news for the Mormons, because it strips them of their false hope and opens the door for you to explain the true gospel that can actually save them. Share with them the hope that is found only in the true Jesus: "For by one offering He has *perfected forever* those who are being sanctified" (Hebrews 10:14).

From Mormonism to Christ

I was a fifth-generation member of the Reorganized Church of Jesus Christ of Latter-Day Saints, formerly known as the "RLDS" church, and now trying to be known as "The Community of Christ" church. The RLDS church is the largest splinter group from the LDS church.

Growing up, my family faithfully followed the way of RLDSism. We considered ourselves very religious. We believed we had the "fullness" of the gospel, because we not only had the Bible, but also possessed the Scriptures in their purest form, the Book of Mormon and the compilation of Joseph Smith's revelations, the Doctrine and Covenants. Growing up, I could never really understand why my Christian friends did not believe I was a Christian, too. Seeking to understand my faith better, I dug into the Book of Mormon and D&C.

My Baptist and Methodist friends often shared the gospel with me, but I could not grasp salvation by grace and faith alone. I could not understand how you could simply say a prayer and then know for sure that your eternal destiny would be heaven, not hell, "regardless of how you lived your life thereafter."

When I would ask my parents about the gospel and what my friends were telling me, they would point me to verses in the New Testament that emphasized how those who "endure to the end will be saved." This didn't really help me, because I obviously was incapable of enduring to the end in a works-based religion. I intuitively understood deep down that I could not work out my salvation based on my own good works. I constantly failed. I couldn't keep my numerous vows "to be good from now on." It became a weight I couldn't bear. I tried to drown out my conscience's promptings and convictions with activities, parties, and living life trying to convince myself that either there was no god (since he didn't seem to hear my prayers to help me live the "right" kind of life) or that I simply couldn't live the kind of life that was necessary to know him intimately on a daily basis.

In the summer of 1989, an RLDS lay-minister spoke at our little small-town RLDS church. He had recently been saved when the Lord showed him his need for repentance and that Jesus had paid for his sins. He was a fourth-generation RLDSer who later became my father-in-law. He shared the good news of the gospel of salvation by grace and faith alone. As he did, the Lord opened the eyes of my heart to fully and finally understand the truth of the pure gospel message. In that instant, I knew that I knew that I knew that I had been fully forgiven, that my eternal destiny had been secured by the pure blood of Jesus alone, and that God loved me regardless of my works. It was literally as if scales fell from eyes, spiritual chains were broken, and the unbearable weight of my guilt had been lifted from me. I was free and I knew it. Tears flooded my eyes. My soul felt as if it were floating at the ceiling of that church that day, lifted up by joy unspeakable and peace that surpasses understanding.

Mormonism is built on the premise that the Bible is not fully reliable due to centuries of adulteration by fallible human scribes. When I experienced new birth, I immediately understood and became convinced that the Bible is true and reliable and that God's Word alone saves.

Since that day, I have had a desire and a passion to share the life-saving, life-transforming message of the pure, unadulterated gospel. I'm so thankful to report that my two brothers, my parents, my grandparents, my wife, her parents, and her siblings are all born-again believers who have left the RLDS church and are now attending great churches. My wife was also a fifth-generation RLDSer.

—Chris T.

Witnessing to a Mormon

You: Hi, guys. Nice bikes.

Marvin: Thanks.

You: Where are you from?

Marvin: Salt Lake City.

You: Nice place. I love the mountains. My name is [your name here].

Marvin: I'm Marvin and this is Erik.

You: Nice to meet you both.

Marvin: Nice to meet you also.

You: I have a question for you. What do you think happens after someone dies?

Marvin: They go to be with Heavenly Father.

You: Everybody?

Marvin: No. Some go to a lower Heaven.

You: Do you think you will go to be with Heavenly Father?

Marvin: I hope so.

You: Do you think that you are good enough to go there?

Marvin: Yes, I believe so. I do my best.

You: Have you kept the Ten Commandments?

Marvin: I think I have.

[If he says that he has broken some of the Commandments, ask which ones. Still go through the Law. You need to *personalize* his sin, as Paul did in Romans 2:21–24.]

You: Let's go through a few of the Commandments to see how you do. How many lies do you think you have told in your whole life? I mean real lies, not just "white" lies.

[Remember to make a distinction between what he perceives as permissible lies and deceitfulness. Otherwise, he may trivialize his lying.]

Marvin: I've told many lies in the past.

You: How many? Ten? Hundreds?

Marvin: Probably a hundred.

You: What do you call someone who tells lies?

Marvin: You would normally call them a "liar." But I've repented.

You: Have you ever stolen anything, in your whole life?

Marvin: Yes, when I was younger.

You: What do you call someone who steals things?

Marvin: A thief.

You: Have you ever used God's name in vain?

Marvin: Plenty of times. I know it's wrong to do that.

You: It certainly is. God gave you life. He gave you eyes to see the beauty of this creation. He gave you ears to enjoy good music, and taste buds to enjoy all the good food. He lavished kindness on you and then you used His holy name as a cuss word. I'm sure you're aware that that's a very serious sin called "blasphemy."

Marvin: You're right.

You: Jesus said, "Who- ever looks at a woman to lust for her has already committed adultery with her in his heart." Have you ever looked with lust?

Marvin: Plenty of times.

You: Then you have committed adultery in God's eyes. So Marvin—and more than likely you, too, Erik—here's a summation of what we have found. You are not a "good" person in God's sight. By your own admission (I'm not judging you), you are a lying, thieving, blasphemous, adulterer at heart.

Marvin: Yes. But I have repented.

You: You have to face God on Judgment Day. If He judges you by the Ten Commandments, will you be innocent or guilty?

Marvin: I will be guilty, if He judges me by the Ten Commandments.

You: Will you go to Heaven or Hell?

Marvin: I will go to Heaven, because I have repented.

You: Did you know that repentance can't help you? That's like standing in front of a good judge and saying, "Judge, I am guilty of raping that woman, but I'm sorry and I won't do it again." The judge is going to say, "You should be sorry because you have done wrong. And of course you shouldn't do it again!" And God is far more righteous than a good judge. The Bible says that He will by no means clear the guilty. Repentance alone cannot save you.

Marvin: Okay. I see what you are saying. But I have also changed my life.

You: You are a criminal in God's sight, and any "good works" you do can't save you because they are actually an attempt to bribe God. So if you died today and God judged you by the Ten Commandments, you would go to Hell—to "outer darkness."

[Don't be afraid to say this, because it's what will get his attention. Works-righteous religions don't give the assurance that true faith in Christ alone gives. There is a hidden fear that the adherent may not be good enough. So, you must use the Law to make sure he realizes that his heart is wicked, that he's sinful by nature, and that there's nothing he can do to make himself "worthy" in the eyes of God. Once he realizes that, then he's ready to hear the gospel, that he can be made perfect through faith in Jesus.]

You: The only way you can be saved from Hell is to trust in Jesus Christ alone.

Marvin: We believe in Jesus. We are called "The Church of Jesus Christ of Latter-day Saints."

You: Is your Jesus the brother of Lucifer?

Marvin: Yes. We believe that.

You: Then the Jesus you believe in is different from the Jesus of the Bible. Besides, your church teaches that His suffering on the cross wasn't enough. Do you remember Jesus' words on the cross—"It is finished!" The debt for *all* sin was paid in full. To be saved, you simply need to trust in Jesus for your salvation, rather than in your good works. Good works should proceed from true faith, but they have no bearing on your salvation. If you died today, you have God's promise that you won't go to Heaven. The Bible warns that all liars will have their part in the lake of fire. No thief, blasphemer, or adulterer will inherit the Kingdom of God.

[Sometimes, when speaking with a Mormon, you may find yourself frustrated and feel that you are at a standstill. If that happens, feel free to say (in a loving, concerned tone), "If the Mormon religion is right and I am wrong, I will go to the third Heaven. But if the Bible is right and you are wrong, you are following a false Jesus that cannot save you, and you will end up in Hell forever."]

Marvin: Yes, but...

You: Give me a moment to share something with you, and then you can give me your thoughts. Okay?

Marvin: Okay.

You: The Bible says that Jesus Christ came to suffer and die for the sin of the world. We broke God's Law (the Ten Commandments) but because Jesus paid our fine on the cross 2,000 years ago, God can forgive us. Jesus became a morally perfect human being and gave His life as a sacrifice for the sin of the world. That means that God can dismiss your case. He can commute your death sentence. The Bible says,

"God demonstrates His own love toward us, in that while we were still sinners, Christ died for us." God proved His great love for you through the cross. Then Jesus rose from the dead and defeated the power of the grave. If you repent and trust the Savior, God will forgive your sins and grant you everlasting life. You will be truly born again, with a new heart and new desires. So, repent—turn from your sin—and trust the Savior alone for your salvation—not in a church or in your good works. Does that make sense?

Marvin: Yes, it does.

You: Guys, thanks for listening to me.

Marvin (and Erik): Thank you.

[It's important to realize that your commission is to preach the gospel to every creature (see Mark 16:15). It is the *gospel* that is the power of God to salvation. You have just done that, so trust in the power of the gospel and in the faithfulness of God to watch over His Word. The results are in His hands. You have sown good seed. God will make it grow, in His perfect time.]

JEHOVAH'S WITNESSES

The Jehovah's Witnesses are best known for their door-to-door evangelism. With over 6 million active Witnesses making house calls each year, there's a very good chance they've knocked on your door at least once.

In fact, no religious group in the world spends as many hours proselytizing as the Jehovah's Witnesses. With followers in 235 countries—1 million in the U.S—they spent over 1.2 *billion* hours in 2005 "proclaiming the good news" of Jehovah and His Kingdom.[3] What motivates them to do what they do? What is the so-called "good news" that they are proclaiming that attracts 300,000 new members each year?

The following information will prepare you so the next time you encounter Jehovah's Witnesses, rather than closing the door in their face, you can be an effective witness for Jesus Christ.

Background

The Jehovah's Witnesses religious movement was started about 130 years ago by a young man named Charles Russell. As a teenager, he left his church because he rejected its biblical teachings on eternal punishment in Hell. So Russell rea-

soned that when man dies, he simply stops existing. He also denied that Jesus was God in human flesh. He didn't believe in the Trinity and many other essential Christian doctrines.

When he was 18 years old, Russell started a Bible study where he began to spread his beliefs. Then he published his own magazine, now known as *The Watchtower*. Some people were fascinated by his "end-of-the-world" predictions, and in 1884 he started the Watchtower Bible and Tract Society, which is headquartered in Brooklyn, New York.

Originally, those who followed Russell were called "Russelites." The name "Jehovah's Witnesses" didn't catch on until almost fifty years later, and is based on Isaiah 43:10, which reads: "Ye are my witnesses, saith Jehovah, and my servant whom I have chosen" (American Standard Version).

The Watchtower Society boldly claims to be the *only* channel of divine truth in the world today, and that no one can be saved apart from their organization.

Scriptures

Since many of their doctrines are easily refuted by the Scriptures, in 1961 the Watchtower Society published their own

Bible. Called the *New World Translation* (NWT), it blatantly alters many verses that revealed the errors of the Watchtower teaching.

In addition, *The Watchtower* magazine is one of their main sources of doctrine. The Watchtower Society teaches that only *they* can interpret the Bible, and no individual can learn the truth apart from them. Jehovah's Witnesses are therefore encouraged to study their Bible *only* in conjunction with the other Watchtower publications, so the Watchtower Society can tell them what it really means.

> "The Bible is an organizational book and belongs to the Christian congregation as an organization, not to individuals, regardless of how sincerely they may believe that they can interpret the Bible. For this reason, the Bible cannot be properly understood without Jehovah's visible organization in mind."[4]

Who Is God?

Jehovah's Witnesses reject the biblical concept of a triune God. Saying that it's "difficult to love and worship a complicated, freakish-looking, three-headed God," they reason that God cannot be a Trinity. After all, God made man in His image, and "no one has ever seen a three-headed human creature" (*Let God Be True*, 2nd ed., pp. 101–102).

Based on Isaiah 43:10, they believe the only true God is known as "Jehovah," the Almighty. Although He is eternal and omnipotent, He is not omnipresent.[5]

In addition, Jehovah's Witnesses deny the deity of the Holy Spirit. They believe the Holy Spirit is not a person but is only "the active force of God" (*Reasoning*, p. 381).

Who Is Jesus?

The Watchtower Society teaches that Jesus is not God incarnate but is just a created being. He is called God's "only begotten Son" because He is the first and only being created directly by Jehovah. As the "first-born of all creation," Jesus was then used by God to create all other things.

Before Jesus came to earth He was Michael the archangel, and is the "second greatest personage of the universe." Through the virgin birth, He was later re-created on earth as a perfect man. Jesus became the Messiah at His baptism, and at that time He was anointed to become the King of the coming Kingdom.

Jehovah's Witnesses also deny the bodily resurrection of Christ. They believe that after Jesus was buried, God disposed of His physical body. Jesus was raised as a *spirit* creature and temporarily "materialized" different physical bodies to make Himself visible to His disciples. Now back in heaven as a spirit, He is once again known as Michael the archangel.[6]

Heaven and Hell

The Watchtower Society denies the existence of Hell as a place of everlasting punishment for the wicked. They argue,

"The doctrine of a burning hell where the wicked are tortured eternally after death cannot be true mainly for four reasons: (1) It is wholly unscriptural; (2) it is unreasonable; (3) it is contrary to God's love; and (4) it is repugnant to justice."[7]

The Jehovah's Witnesses (like the Seventh-Day Adventists) believe in "soul sleep": that humans don't have immortal souls, so when the body dies there is no longer any conscience existence. They teach that Hell, or Sheol, is simply the common grave of mankind. From there, those who are righteous will be resurrected; those who are ultimately condemned by God will be annihilated and cease to exist.

The Watchtower theology of Heaven is based on their interpretation of the Book of Revelation. They teach that when the saints go marching in, you're not going to be in that number because the only ones who will enter the Pearly Gates are the 144,000 "anointed ones." According to the Watchtower, all of these 144,000 "tickets" to Heaven have already been "sold out." Only these 144,000 are born again, are members of the spiritual body of Christ, and can expect to reign with Christ in Heaven.

So for the vast majority of remaining Jehovah's Witnesses, known as the "other sheep" or the "great crowd," Christ's sacrifice provides only a chance at eternal life on earth.[8] They will never go to Heaven or see Jesus/Michael. Their only hope is to live in the Paradise established on earth after Armageddon.

These "other sheep" expect to be given a physical *eternal life* on earth, in contrast to *immortality* as spirits in Heaven for the 144,000.

Note that, like the Mormon church, Jehovah's Witnesses redefine biblical words, making it difficult to witness to them. You can try to convince them that "unless one is born again, he cannot see the kingdom of God" (John 3:3), and they'll agree with you. They believe only the 144,000 who are born-again will go to "the kingdom of God," while they're content to end up in Paradise on earth—therefore, they don't need to be born again.

Sin and Salvation

Jehovah's Witnesses believe that in the Fall, all mankind inherited "imperfection" from Adam and Eve and hence are sinners who are subject to death. But they believe sin was only *partially* atoned for by Christ. As a perfect man, Christ's death paid the ransom that removed the effects of *Adam's* sin, but individuals still have to work to earn forgiveness for *their* present and future sins. In other words, original sin that brought death was canceled by Christ's atonement—yet men can still die by their own rebellion and sin.

For Jehovah's Witnesses, salvation requires a complicated combination of belief and good works:

"[Belief] involves taking in accurate knowledge of God's purposes and his way of salvation. Then faith has to be exercised in Jesus Christ as the Chief Agent of salvation...This places the Christian in a saved condition, but he must now persevere in doing God's will and continue to adhere to all of God's requirements for the rest of his life. Only then will he be saved to eternal life."[9]

Jehovah is said to be a God of "grace" only because without Jesus' death for our sins, no one would have the *opportunity* to merit salvation. In addition to faith in Jesus' sacrifice, requirements for salvation include baptism by immersion, repentance, active association with the Watchtower Society, righteous conduct, and absolute loyalty to Jehovah. Even then, there is no assurance of salvation, only hope for a resurrection. Those who fail to live up to these requirements, or who are disfellowshipped by the Watchtower Society, have no hope of salvation.

Jehovah's Witnesses are told that serving as loyal spokesmen for the Society is "a sacred duty, a requirement on which our life depends."[10] Witnesses are compelled to knock on door after door to try to spread their beliefs—and earn their salvation.

Witnesses are expected to spend five hours a week going door-to-door, to sell twelve subscriptions to *The Watchtower* magazine each month, and to conduct a monthly "Bible study" in the homes of their converts.[11] They then have to submit detailed reports of their activity, and their performance will affect their status in the local congregation or "Kingdom Hall"—adding more pressure for them to work harder. With a lifetime of works to try to earn their salvation, it's hard to see how their gospel is "good news" at all.

Jehovah's Witness Customs

No crosses: Because Jehovah's Witnesses teach that Jesus was executed on a "torture stake," they reject the traditional symbol of Christianity, the cross, as being of pagan origin. They believe displaying a cross (whether on a necklace or church) is idol worship—so you won't see any on their buildings.

Forbidden activities: The Watchtower Society also forbids many activities that are not explicitly forbidden in the Bible: such as smoking, blood transfusions, boxing, or participating in a raffle, as well as things related to the current earthly kingdom, like saluting the flag, reciting the Pledge of Allegiance, standing for or singing the national anthem, voting, and performing military or civic service. The Society also forbids celebrating personal birthdays, Christmas, Easter, Mother's Day and Father's Day, as well as most other holidays, believing that they have pagan roots.

No association: So that Jehovah's Witnesses are not corrupted by contact with others, they are not allowed to associate with non-Witnesses—even those in their own family. The only exception is if a non-Witness family member is living in the same household.[12]

How to Reach a Jehovah's Witness

As you're talking with Jehovah's Witnesses, keep in mind that they believe they worship the true God of the Bible, while Christians are lost souls who have been misled by the devil into worshipping a pagan three-headed deity. So don't be surprised if they're not very receptive to your message.

Also keep in mind that members are taught to obediently follow all the teachings of their leaders, and any who question their teaching are severely reprimanded or even disfellowshipped. Because a member who leaves the organization must be shunned by all other Witnesses—including his family—he's not going to give up his beliefs easily.

So what's the best way to reach a Jehovah's Witness? Should you try to convince him that Jesus is God, or of the existence of Hell? Well, if you have the confidence to, try it. Many ex-Witnesses say they were forced to reexamine their beliefs because someone planted just one seed of doubt in their minds about the truthfulness of the Watchtower teachings. The Word of God is living and powerful, and *will* have an impact.

If you can quickly demonstrate from Scripture that Jesus is God, Jehovah's Witnesses will have to reconsider their understanding of God. They will now have two Persons who are God—Father and Son. For example, have them read Isaiah 7:14 and 9:6. Point out that the Messiah would be "Immanuel" ("God with us") and would be called "Mighty God"—the same name used for Jehovah in Isaiah 10:21.

But a word of caution: Be careful you don't try to win the fight simply by arguing doctrine—and then failing to share the gospel biblically. If you don't address the conscience, you'll end up trapped in the intellect with nowhere to go.

So next time the Jehovah's Witnesses come calling, take the opportunity to speak with them. Don't worry about straightening out all the areas of disagreement, but gently point them to the moral Law, the Ten Commandments. Show them that as lawbreakers they will be guilty before a holy God, and that no amount of works will ever save them.

And remember—those who are caught in this cult are spending one billion hours spreading their false teaching. Be sure you're a faithful witness for the Lord Jesus Christ and spend your time wisely in spreading what is truly "good news"!

From Jehovah's Witnesses to Christ

Born and raised as a Jehovah's Witness (JW), it was the life I lived up until my early thirties. I left Jehovah's Witnesses because their faith is based on works and fear. I struggled growing up with this for years. I feared displeasing God but most of all His people. The thought of even questioning the flaws of this organization could categorize me as taking sides with the enemy, an apostate view. I didn't want to lose my family.

But I couldn't seem to measure up, no matter how hard I tried serving the Lord. I felt like a prisoner living in fear of God and destruction if I didn't keep up with the rules. I had the Bible knowledge in my head, but didn't really have the heart knowledge. The fruit of the Holy Spirit seemed to be missing at times. That's when I knew something was wrong. Why did this belief of JWs not always permeate the heart, soul, and mind in others and myself? Why did I feel like a robot attending these meetings? How could I question the people who seemed to have God's tools, the Bible and prayer? Weren't they imperfect, too? Weren't they capable of grieving the Holy Spirit? Why did I feel I was on a tread-mill serving the Lord? I felt I was being examined and constantly under surveillance like a mouse in a lab experiment. Was this God's plan for me?

Some years ago, a friend invited me to her church to hear a Christian band. Once I was there, the Lord used a prayer ministry at this church to transform my lie-based thinking into a loving, personal, intimate relationship with Him. I've been delivered from the loneliness of guilt and condemnation and adopted into the Body of Christ. I'm a work in progress, but now I serve the Lord with love, not out of obligation and fear.

I discovered in my journey with the Lord that I was really afraid of my Father in heaven. I really didn't know God in an intimate, personal way. Nor did I really know the depths of grace through His Son, Jesus Christ. I was truly lost and con-fused. Then, Jesus rescued me and took all the guilt, doubts, and heavy burdens I held inside. I'm now allowing Him to teach me all over again. I'm not afraid of being cor-rected or disciplined by my Heavenly Father. I can come to Him and even His Body when I'm struggling with an issue and not feel condemned but convicted in spirit and truth.

Now I know that God is all-powerful and full of grace and mercy. I know what He's done for me through the power of His blood and sacrifice. I'm embraced in the arms of God's grace and love feeling secure and blessed. The

> most important thing Jesus has taught me is that He will never reject me. God is my Father in Heaven, my safe haven. I'm no longer alone. I have an adopted family called the Body of Christ. I can serve God anywhere and it doesn't have to be in a building of JWs.
> —*Liesl V.*

Witnessing to a Jehovah's Witness

(Knock-knock.)

You: Hello.

[There are two people at your door, carrying magazines, books, and cases. They are obviously JWs so make sure you are very friendly right from the beginning. They normally get a cold response. So be very warm.]

John: Hello, I'm John and this is Bob. We are in the area talking to people about spiritual things.

You: Interesting. My name is [your name here]. Pleased to meet you.

John: Good to meet you too.

You: Are you Jehovah's Witnesses?

John: Yes, we are.

You: I have a question for you. I have a knife in my back and I have only three minutes to live. How can I enter the Kingdom?

John: Three minutes! Wow. Well, you have to live a good life, learn of Jehovah, go door to door, help people, pray, etc.

You: I can't *do* anything. I have a knife in my back. And I can't live a good life. I have lied, stolen, I'm a fornicator and a blasphemer. I now have two minutes. Help me!

John: Um...

You: One minute to live. Can you help me? How can I enter the Kingdom?

John: Sorry. We can't help you.

You: John, think of the thief on the cross. He said that he was justly condemned. I don't think he was thinking that Roman law was just in executing him. Justice for a thief is normally a few months in prison, not capital punishment. I think he was speaking of *God's* Law. It justly condemned him. He couldn't *do* anything to be saved. He couldn't go anywhere; his hands and his feet were pinned to the cross. Let me ask you a question: Do you think that you are a good person?

[Even though Jehovah's Witnesses believe that Jesus died on a torture stake, we should still preach the cross. This is because it is part of the truth of the gospel. We should also preach sin and Hell to those who believe in neither. If they object and say that it was a stake, don't let it become a point of contention.]

John: Yes, I do.

You: Do you think you have kept the Ten Commandments?

John: I think I have. I try to.

You: Let's go through a few of the Commandments to see how you do. How many lies do you think you have told in your whole life? I mean real lies, not just "white" lies.

[Remember to make a distinction between what he perceives as permissible lies and deceitfulness.]

John: I've probably told many lies in my life.

You: How many do you think? Five? Ten?

John: Maybe twenty or thirty.

You: What do you call someone who tells lies?

John: A liar. But it was in the past. I've repented and changed my life.

[Don't be concerned that the Jehovah's Witness believes he has reformed his ways and is living a good life. He is still trusting in his own goodness to save him, and you have to show him that his righteous deeds are filthy and putrid in the sight of a holy God: "But we are all like an unclean thing, and all our righteousnesses are like filthy rags; we all fade as a leaf; and our iniquities, like the wind, have taken us away" (Isaiah 64:6).]

You: We often think lightly of lying, calling lies fibs or "white lies," but the Bible tells us that "lying lips are an abomination to the Lord." That means lies are "extremely detestable" to Him. Have you ever stolen anything, in your whole life?

John: Yes, I have, but that was years ago. Like I said, I've changed.

You: Stay with me, John. What do you call someone who steals things?

John: A thief.

You: Have you ever used God's name in vain?

John: Yes. I used to do that.

You: Think about that. Jehovah gave you life. He gave you eyes to see the beauty of this creation. He gave you ears to enjoy good music, taste buds to enjoy good food. He lavished His goodness upon you, and then you used His holy name as a cuss word to express disgust. That's a very serious sin—one that is called "blasphemy."

John: You're right.

You: Jesus said, "Whoever looks at a woman to lust for her has already committed adultery with her in his heart." Have you ever looked with lust?

John: Yes, sir, I have.

You: Then you have committed adultery in God's eyes. So, John, here's a summary of what we have found. You are not the "good" person you thought you were. By your own admission (I'm not judging you), you are a lying, thieving, blasphemous, adulterer at heart. And you have to face God on Judgment Day. If He judges you by the Ten Commandments, will you be innocent or guilty?

John: If it's by the Ten Commandments, I will be guilty.

You: Will you go to Heaven or Hell?

John: I think I would go to Hell, if they are the only two choices.

[The introduction of the Law of God often deals with the falsehood that "Hell" is merely the grave. The moral Law makes a literal Hell reasonable.]

You: You and I are criminals in God's sight, and any good works we do can't save us. Our "good works" are in essence an attempt to bribe God. We are in exactly the same predicament as the thief on the cross. Remember, he couldn't go anywhere or "do" anything—he was nailed to a cross. We too are guilty criminals who have broken the Ten Commandments, and God's Law nails us also. That leaves us with the only alternative the thief had—to be saved by grace through faith alone in Jesus. He "turned" to Jesus. That's what we must do through repentance. Then he said, "Lord, remember me..." He therefore believed that Jesus was Lord, and that He was going to rise from the dead, which are the requirements for salvation (see Romans 10:9,10). We must do the same. Jesus suffered and died on the cross, taking the punishment for our sins. We broke the Law, and Jesus paid our fine in His life's blood. That means, because of the suffering death and resurrection of Jesus Christ, God can now dismiss our case. He can commute our death sentence and allow us to live. What we must do is repent, and trust in Him *alone* (not in our works) for our eternal salvation. Hey, John, thanks for listening to me.

John: You're welcome.

[Don't be discouraged if you don't see any visible results. Sometimes the person to whom you are witnessing may even agree with you by saying, "Yes, we are saved by grace through faith in Jesus." If you don't keep in mind that he is speaking a different language from you, it may take the wind out of your sails. Remember, his definition of "grace" and "saved" are completely different from the biblical definitions, so make sure you explain the difference between their "gospel" and the one taught by the Bible.

Charles Spurgeon said, "I have heard it said that if there is a crooked stick, and you want to show how crooked it is, you need not waste words in description. Place a straight one by the side of it, and the thing is done directly." That's what you are doing by preaching the truth. Again, go straight to the conscience. Do what Jesus did. Open up the Commandments and help him see sin in its true light. He must see that God is angry with him, that he's in terrible danger, and that he *cannot* save himself. Don't worry if you're not an "expert" in the beliefs of Jehovah's Witnesses. If you have planted the seed of the true gospel into their hearts, you have succeeded. The rest is up to God.]

Food for Thought

Because Charles Russell rejected the idea of eternal torment in Hell, what if he had formed his new theology by reasoning along these lines?

1. There is no eternal torment in Hell for unbelievers.

2. If, after this life, there is no torment for the unbeliever, then there must not be any conscious existence for the unbeliever either. Therefore, man cannot have a soul that is immortal.

3. If, when one dies, one's existence ceases, then when Jesus Christ died, He ceased to exist. If Jesus ceased to exist when He died, then He cannot be God, for God cannot cease to exist.

4. If Jesus is not God, then God does not exist eternally in three Persons: Father, Son, and Holy Spirit. Thus, the Trinity is a false teaching.[13]

What a tragic conclusion, which he used to start a new religion that has managed to deceive millions! Imagine what might have happened instead if the church he attended as a youth had simply made Hell seem reasonable. If they had used the Law, as God intended, to show sin to be exceedingly sinful . . .

ISLAM

With approximately 1.5 billion adherents, Islam is the world's second largest religion. It is also both the youngest of the major world religions, and the fastest growing religion today. It's amazing to think about, but one of every five people in the world is a Muslim. Christianity is currently the largest religion, followed by one-third of the world's population. But if current trends continue, Islam will become the most popular world religion sometime in the mid-21st century.

Despite the Middle East being the birthplace of Islam, the majority of Muslims (about 75%) are non-Arabs. Although we hear a lot about Muslims in the news, most of us don't know much about their beliefs or how to reach them with the gospel. As with most religions, Islam has some similarities with Christianity, but it's the differences that we want to consider.

Background

Approximately 1,500 years ago in Mecca, Saudi Arabia, a man named Muhammad was contemplating inside a cave when he claimed he was visited by an angel named Gabriel. The angel gave him messages, and continued to reveal things to him over a 23-year period. Muhammad used these teachings to form the basis of a religion called Islam.

The word "Islam" means "surrender" or "submission." People who believe the teachings of Islam are known as Muslims.

Yet Muslims do not believe that Muhammad and his followers were the first Muslims. Others mentioned in the Bible—such as Abraham (Koran, 3:67)—were Muslims, even though they lived hundreds of years before Muhammad.

In fact, Muslims believe that Islam was the original religion from the time of creation, and that Adam was the first prophet of Allah. Other biblical characters such as Noah, Moses, David, Solomon, John the Baptist, and Jesus were also prophets of Allah. In all, there have been about 124,000 prophets sent for specific times, but Muhammad is considered the last and the greatest, and is known as the "seal of the prophets."

After Muhammad's death, his followers disagreed on who should be his successor, and they divided into two main groups: the Sunnis and the Shi'ites. About 85 percent of the world's Muslims are Sunnis and 15 percent are Shi'ites. The two branches differ somewhat in their practices and traditions.

Scriptures

Muslims believe their holy book, the Koran (or Quran), was dictated to the Muslim prophet Muhammad by an angel from Allah. Muhammad recited the messages to his followers, who either wrote the words down or memorized them. The Koran was not arranged into the form of a book until after Muhammad's death. Sometime later, a Muslim leader collected all the writings that were part of the official Koran, and he ordered other versions to be burned.

The Koran is divided into 114 chapters, called suras, which cover the topics of ethics, history, law, and theology. It is slightly smaller than the New Testament. Although the Koran is printed in many languages, Muslims believe Arabic is the language of Allah, and that the true meaning of the Koran can be fully learned only in Arabic. Muslims who memorize the Koran usually memorize it in Arabic, even if they don't understand the language. Because they believe it is the word of Allah, Muslims handle copies of the Koran with great care. They wash their hands before reading it, and they keep it in a safe place—never on the floor. In Muslim countries, anyone who intentionally damages a Koran can be arrested.

Islam teaches that Allah was the source of both the Bible and the Koran. Muslims believe that some of the previous prophets were given books that are considered to be divinely inspired:

1) The *Tawrat* (Torah), given to Moses

2) The *Zabur* (Psalms), given to David

3) The *Injil* (Gospel), given to Jesus

4) The Koran, given to Muhammad

Muslims are taught that the first three have been cor-rupted, so to correct the errors Allah appointed Muhammad to receive the Koran. It supersedes all previous revelation, and Allah has preserved it from corruption. (Perhaps this would be a good question to ask a Muslim: If all books were originally true and given by Allah, who is able to preserve his word, why is he able to keep the Koran free from corruption, but he wasn't able to preserve the first three?)

In addition, Muslims try to live as Muhammad did by following the *hadith*, collections of records of the things Muhammad and his companions did and said. Several *hadith* collectors gathered reports of Muhammad's life, similar to the different Gospel accounts of Jesus' life.

Who Is God?

Like in Christianity and Judaism, Islam teaches monotheism—a belief that there is only one God. Muslims worship Allah, who they believe created the universe in six days and is in complete control of all things. While he is eternal, omnipotent, omnipresent, and omniscient, Muslims believe that Allah himself is not knowable, and they cannot have a personal relationship with him. Rather than fellowship with Allah, Islam is concerned only with allegiance to him and total submission to his will.

The Koran does not say that Allah seeks to redeem those lost in sin, and it states repeatedly that he does not love sinners (Sura 3:32; 4:107).

The Muslim belief that there are no gods other than Allah is recited daily in the *shahada*. Like with Judaism, they believe in God's absolute oneness and reject the Trinity.

To ascribe any partners to Allah is to commit the unforgivable sin of *shirk*.

Who Is Jesus?

Muslims believe that, prior to Muhammad, Allah sent many great prophets who spoke for God to specific people, and whose message was meant for that time. Jesus, then, was simply one of many prophets according to Islam. The Koran does acknowledge Jesus' virgin birth, holy life, and many miracles, but says He was no more than a man. Jesus (whom they call Isa) must never be called "God," "Lord," or the "Son of God." The Koran has many verses stating that Jesus is not the son of Allah, and adds that anyone who says Allah has a son is a liar (Sura 37:152). Many Muslims think calling Jesus "the Son of God" means that Allah had physical relations, which is highly offensive.

The Koran teaches that Jesus did not die, but was taken directly to heaven. Muslims believe that Allah would not allow Jesus, a prophet, to die on the cross. Such a death would mean defeat—if Jesus were killed, that would mean He failed and His enemies won. So they believe someone else, possibly Judas, was made to look like Jesus and died on the cross in place of Jesus. Of course, since they believe Jesus didn't die, then He also did not rise from the dead.

Heaven and Hell

Muslims believe that everyone will attain either the punishment of Hell or the reward of Heaven (Paradise).

"For those who reject Allah, is a terrible Penalty: but for those who believe and work righteous deeds, is Forgiveness, and a magnificent Reward." (Sura 35:7)

Hell is where unbelievers and sinners will spend eternity. One translation of the Koran states: "The unbelievers among the People of the Book [Christians and Jews] and the pagans shall burn for ever in the fire of Hell. They are the vilest of all creatures" (Sura 98:1–8).

The "magnificent reward" that Muslims hope to achieve is Paradise—"gardens of bliss" where they will be joined by their spouses (resurrected as virgins) and waited on by immortal youths. There they will enjoy sensual pleasures: choice food and drink, nice clothes and jewelry, lovely companions, and beautiful virgins (Sura 56:12–37).

Sin and Salvation

Muslims believe human beings are born sinless and are good by nature. Since they don't have a fallen nature, they don't think they need a Savior. They depend on their own efforts to please Allah.

Muslims believe that Allah will judge everyone on Judgment Day according to their deeds (helping others, testifying to the truth of God, leading a virtuous life). If they have done more good deeds than bad, they hope Allah will forgive their sins and let them into Paradise when they die. But they can't be sure.

The Koran tells them that the good deeds they do will cancel out bad deeds (Sura 11:114), but no one knows how many good deeds are enough. Although they believe they can ask Allah to forgive their sins, Allah may or may not forgive them. The Koran says, "Allah ... punishes whom he pleases and forgives whom he pleases" (Sura 5:40).

Because the tally of good deeds vs. bad is known only to Allah, Muslims cannot know whether they are saved until Judgment Day. The Koran says:

> "Then those whose balance (of good deeds) is heavy, they will be successful. But those whose balance is light, will be those who have lost their souls; in hell will they abide." (Sura 23:102–103)

To go to Paradise, the Koran says Muslims should believe in Allah, the prophets of Islam, the Koran, angels, and Judgment Day (Sura 4:136). They must repent and obey Islamic law, but even doing those things will not necessarily assure Muslims of salvation.

In other words, though Allah is frequently called Forgiving and Merciful in the Koran, forgiveness and mercy don't appear to be applied to the sinner's account—sin must still be atoned for by each individual's works.

Muslim Customs

All Muslims have five important duties that they are obligated to fulfill. These duties, called the "Five Pillars," are referred to by their Arabic names:

1. *Shahada*: Confess the faith by reciting, "There is no God but Allah, and Muhammad is his messenger."

2. *Salat*: Pray five times a day at specific times while facing the city of Mecca, the birthplace of Muhammad. Wherever they live, all Muslims must face Mecca during their times of prayer, and perform ceremonial washing beforehand. The five daily prayers are recited in Arabic.

3. *Zakat*: Give money to help the poor. Muslim adults are required to give 2.5 percent of their wealth to charity every year. Some Muslim youth do volunteer work as a form of helping the needy.

4. *Sawm*: Fast from sunrise to sunset during the Muslim holy month of Ramadan, to remember the giving of the Koran to Muhammad. After sunset, Muslims may get together with family and friends to eat a meal called *iftar*. Muslims celebrate the end of Ramadan with a three-day festival called *Eid al-Fitr*. Schools and businesses close in Muslim countries for the holidays.

5. *Hajj*: Take a pilgrimage to Mecca at least once if possible. Mecca is a holy city for Muslims; by law, non-Muslims may not enter it. On the road to Mecca, highway signs direct non-Muslims to exit before reaching the city. Once a year, approximately 2 million Muslims from all over the world come to Mecca for the *Hajj*, a ritual lasting several days. For many Muslims, the *Hajj* is the high point of their lives.

The Five Pillars form the framework for the Muslim's life and practice. Faithfully adhering to these pillars is how Muslims hope to satisfy Allah and achieve salvation.

Tips for Witnessing

- Often Christians feel that it's their job to try to explain the deity of Jesus to a Muslim. However, keep in mind these verses: "He said to them, 'But who do you say that I am?' Simon Peter answered and said, 'You are the Christ, the Son of the living God.' Jesus answered and said to him, 'Blessed are you, Simon Bar-Jonah, for flesh and blood has not revealed this to you, *but My Father who is in heaven*" (Matthew 16:15–17, emphasis added). Let God reveal to him who Jesus is.

- Also, it's not wise to try to explain the Trinity unless the person brings it up. Keep in mind that in Islam, the greatest of sins, called *shirk*, is to attribute "partners" to God. To say that God is a Trinity of persons is an unforgivable sin to a Muslim.

- Muslims have the highest regard for their Koran—keeping it above their waist, placing it on the highest shelf, and never letting it touch the ground. If you witness to them using a marked-up, highlighted Bible, they will consider it very irreverent and disrespectful.

- Muslims believe Allah punishes people for their own sins. Many believe it would be unfair for Jesus to be punished and to die for the sins of others. C. S. Lewis suggests thinking about sins as if they were debts. It makes sense for those in debt to seek help from someone who owes nothing and can afford to help those who do. Jesus did not sin, so He is able to help those who come to Him for salvation from their sins.

How to Reach Muslims

Before you witness to a Muslim, it is important to make sure that he understands that repentance and being sorry for sin will not help him when he faces God on Judgment Day. So make sure you take the time to give the following analogy (you will regret it if you don't). Tell him that a criminal has committed a *very* serious crime. It is so serious that there is a two-million-dollar fine. The criminal says, "Judge, I'm guilty, but I'm sorry for what I've done, and I won't do it again." Is the judge going to therefore let him go? Of course not! If the judge is a good man, he must make sure that justice is done. He can't just let the man leave because he's sorry (he should be sorry because he broke the law, and of course he shouldn't do it again).

The fine must be paid, or the man goes to prison. Make sure he understands this. Go over it again with him. Try to get him to say, "Yes, I understand. That makes sense. Being sorry and saying that he won't break the law again will not help him."

Then ask him if he thinks that he will make it to Heaven—is he a good person? Take him through the Ten Commandments. You will find that it's often like pulling teeth to get him to admit that he has lusted or lied, but stay with it. Try to keep it light. Smile with unbelief if he says that he has never looked with lust. What he is trying to do is trivialize his sin.

Let me explain what happened to Danny, a friend of mine. When he told me that he once went to prison for failing to pay parking tickets, I asked, "Why didn't you just pay them?" He answered, "They were just parking tickets; it was no big deal."

Then he told me that the police arrived at his home at 4:00 a.m., put him in a big black bus and took him to Los Angeles County courts. As he stood before the judge, he said, "Your honor. I brought $700 with me to pay the tickets and to cover the court costs." The judge said, "Mr. Goodall. I'm going to save you all that money. You are going to jail!" Danny was terrified.

His big mistake was that he trivialized his crimes by thinking that they were "just" parking tickets, and so he deceived himself. Had he known the judge's ruling (that he would go to prison), he would have immediately made things right between himself and the law.

Most of us realize that we have broken God's Law, the Ten Commandments, but think it's no big deal. When asked if we have lied, we will say, "Yes. But they were only white lies. They were nothing serious." When asked, "Have you ever stolen something?" we say, "Yes, but only little things." We trivializing the crimes, and like Danny, we deceive ourselves. What we are saying is that we haven't actually "sinned," and the Bible warns, "He who says he has no sin deceives himself." The truth is, if I have lied then I am a liar. If I have stolen anything (the value of the item stolen is irrelevant), I am a thief.

What we need to hear is the judge's ruling for lying and stealing. Here it is: "All liars will have their part in the lake of fire." All liars go to Hell. If the sinner says, "I don't believe in Hell," that's like my friend saying to the judge, "I don't believe in jail." What we believe or don't believe doesn't change reality. No thief will enter Heaven. Not one. Now look at this: Jesus said, "Whoever looks at a woman to lust for her has already committed adultery with her in his heart" (Matthew 5:28).

A man in a rowboat once found himself caught in fast-moving water, heading for a massive waterfall with jagged rocks 150 feet below. A passerby saw him rowing against the current, but his efforts were futile. Minute by minute the boat was drawn closer and closer to the roaring falls. The bystander ran to his car, grabbed a rope from the trunk, and threw it to the boat. When it fell across the bow, he screamed, "Grab the rope. I will pull you to the shore!" He couldn't believe his eyes. The man took no notice. He just kept rowing frantically against the current, until he was sucked over the falls to his death.

The Bible tells us that we cannot "do" anything for our salvation. But God Himself did something wonderful to save us from death and Hell. He became a person in Jesus Christ, and suffered and died in our place. He paid the fine in His life's blood for the crimes that we committed: "God demonstrates His own love toward us, in that while we were still sinners, Christ died for us." Then He rose from the dead and defeated death.

Now here's the difference between being a Muslim and a Christian. There are millions of people on this earth who have never seen the serious nature of sin. They are in the dark about the Judge's ruling. They have no idea that they will end up in Hell for crimes that they consider trivial. They know that they have to face God after death, but they think that their religious works (like Danny with his $700) will buy their way out of any trouble in which they may find themselves. And as long as they trivialize their sin, they will deceive themselves into thinking that they can work their way into Heaven by their religious works. But it is as futile as the man who tried to row against the river until he went over the falls.

God Himself has thrown us a rope in Jesus Christ. He is the only One who can save us from death and Hell. But we must let go of our own efforts to save ourselves and take hold of the rope. The moment we cease our own religious "rowing" and have faith in Jesus, that is when we find peace with God.

Witnessing to a Muslim

You: Hi, my name is [your name here].

Ehud: I'm Ehud.

You: Pleased to meet you, Ehud. Do you like driving taxis?

Ehud: I guess I must. I've been doing it for ten years.

You: Hey, Ehud, I have a question for you. What do you think happens when someone dies? Where do they go?

Ehud: They go to Paradise. Or some people go to Hell.

You: Where are you going?

Ehud: I don't know. Paradise, I hope.

You: There is an easy way to find out, Ehud. Before I share it with you, let me ask you a question.

Ehud: Okay.

You: A criminal has committed a *very* serious crime. It is so serious that there is a two-million-dollar fine. He says, "Judge, I'm guilty, but I'm sorry for what I've done, and I won't do it again." Is the judge going to therefore let him go?

Ehud: Definitely not.

You: That's right. If the judge is a good man, he must make sure that justice is done. He can't just let the guilty man go because he's sorry. The criminal *should* be sorry because he broke the law, and of course he shouldn't do it again. Does that make sense?

Ehud: Yes, of course.

You: So if a man has seriously broken the law, it's not enough for him to be sorry and to say he won't do it again. If a judge just let him go because of that, he wouldn't be a good judge.

Ehud: That's right. He cannot let him go.

You: So, Ehud, do you think that you are a good person?

Ehud: Yes, I am.

You: Have you kept the Law of Moses, the Ten Commandments?

Ehud: Yes, I think I have kept most of them.

You: Let's go through a few to see how you do. How many lies do you think you have told, in your whole life? I don't mean "white" lies—real lies.

[Again, if you don't make a distinction between what he perceives as permissible lies and deceitfulness, he will trivialize his lying, so get an admission from him that he has actually borne false witness.]

Ehud: I have told some.

You: Two? Ten? Hundreds?

Ehud: Maybe a few dozen.

You: What do you call someone who tells lies?

Ehud: I don't call them anything.

You: What would you call *me* if I told lies?

Ehud: You would be a liar.

You: Ehud, we often think lightly of lying, calling them fibs or "white lies," yet the Scriptures tell us that "lying lips are an abomination to the Lord." That means lies are "extremely detestable" to Him.

You: Have you ever stolen anything, in your whole life?

Ehud: Yes, I have, when I was a young man.

You: What do you call someone who steals things?

Ehud: He is a thief.

You: Have you ever used God's name in vain?

Ehud: Never.

You: The prophet Jesus said, "Whoever looks at a woman to lust for her has already committed adultery with her in his heart." Have you ever done that?

Ehud: What do you mean?

You: Lusted after a woman . . . had sexual desire for her.

Ehud: No.

You: Are you a homosexual?

Ehud: No, I'm not!

You: So, Ehud, have you lusted after a woman?

Ehud: Yes, I have, many times.

You: Here then is a summary of what we have found. By your own admission (I'm not judging you), you are a lying, thieving, blasphemous, adulterer at heart.

Ehud: But I tell God I am sorry. I repent.

You: That won't help you. Remember the story about the criminal who said he was sorry and he wouldn't do it again, and how a good judge couldn't let him go?

Ehud: But God is different.

You: That's right. He's even more righteous than an earthly judge. He will by no means clear the guilty. So when you stand before Him on Judgment Day, will you be innocent or guilty?

Ehud: I suppose I will be guilty.

You: Will you go to Heaven or Hell?

Ehud: I will go to Heaven.

You: Why?

Ehud: Because I am a good person.

You: In *your* eyes you are a good person, and even in my eyes you seem like a really nice guy. But on Judgment Day you have to face a holy God who demands moral perfection —in thought, word, and I deed. So, when did you last lust after a woman?

Ehud: A few minutes ago. Okay, I see what you are saying…

You: The Bible warns that all liars will have their part in the lake of fire. No thief or adulterer will inherit the Kingdom of God. Does it concern you that if you died right now, you would go to Hell, forever?

Ehud: Yes, it does.

You: So, do you know what God did for us, so that we could avoid Hell?

Ehud: No. What did He do?

[Be careful not to say that God had a Son, or that Jesus was God manifest in the flesh. Just preach Christ crucified.]

You: Think of that courtroom story. The criminal couldn't pay the fine. He was in big trouble, when someone he didn't even know stepped in and paid the fine for him. Now that judge can let him go because the fine has been paid—justice has been served. We broke God's Law (the Ten Commandments) but because Jesus paid our fine on the cross 2,000 years ago in His life's blood, God can now forgive us. He can dismiss your case. He can commute your death sentence. The Bible says, "God demonstrates His own love toward us, in that while we were still sinners, Christ died for us." God proved His great love for you through the cross. Then Jesus rose from the dead, and defeated the power of the grave. If you repent and trust the Savior, God will forgive your sins and grant you everlasting life. Does that make sense to you?

Ehud: Yes, it does. I have never heard that before.

You: Ehud, if you died today, where would you go—where would you spend eternity? Think carefully before you answer. This is so important.

Ehud: I would go to Hell.

You: Really? So what are you going to do about it?

Ehud: I think I need to pray.

You: Yes, and repent and trust the Savior. When are you going to do that?

Ehud: I will do that today. Right now. Thank you for talking to me.

From Islam to Christ

I was born in Turkey, and was raised as a Muslim. Islam was my belief, culture, and identity. I never had a doubt about Islam. I believed in the Koran and the last prophet with all my heart.

I wanted to be a Muslim, not because I was born in a Muslim family but because Islam is the truth. Therefore, I decided to learn about other religions. I was wondering why other people do not believe in Islam. I looked for people who believe in different religions.

I read the Koran, and I was stunned when I read that Christians will go to Hell directly because they make Jesus equal to God! (See, e.g., "They surely disbelieve who say: Lo! Allah is the Messiah, son of Mary. The Messiah (himself) said: O Children of Israel, worship Allah, my Lord and your Lord. Lo! whoso ascribeth partners unto Allah, *for him Allah hath forbidden Paradise. His abode is the Fire.* For evil-doers there will be no helpers" [Qur'an, 5:72]). I could not understand that. Isn't it God's religion? Didn't God send Jesus? Why did God send Jesus who seems like a useless prophet who could not teach?

Jesus could not complete his mission as a prophet, people misunderstood him by calling him God, and at the end God had to save him from crucifixion. So why did God send Jesus?

I felt sorry about my Christian friends. I thought I should learn about Christianity so that I could help my Christian friends.

I bought a New Testament, and started reading. My real purpose was to find the mistakes. I did not start from the beginning. I began reading some chapters in the letters. As I was reading, I really liked the idea that when you marry your body belongs to your spouse, and his/her body belongs to you. I saw that the New Testament gives great importance to the women (it is not making them second-class people). And I realized that I might not find mistakes but become very interested in Christianity. Therefore, I stopped reading that book.

One day my friend told me that he had a Christian friend who talks about Jesus. I asked his phone number and called him. He invited me to a Christian meeting at the church. When I went there I saw that there were Christian Turks at that meeting. I could not believe that because how could a Turk become a Christian in a country in which they could easily learn about Islam? I thought that these Christian Turks were socially weak and could not exist by themselves, therefore they were involved in such an activity.

However, I enjoyed going to these meetings because I

could ask questions and discuss about religions. The second week I also invited my best friend to this meeting.

One day, this Christian friend invited me and my best friend to his house to watch a movie called *Jesus*. During the movie I expected that Jesus would say, "A prophet will come after me and you shall believe in him." Surprisingly, he did not say that.

I realized that the Christianity I discovered was different from the one I thought I knew. This time, I started reading the New Testament again. When I read the New Testament, I realized that I have to believe either Jesus or Mohammed. Jesus said he is the only way. But Mohammed said he is the last prophet.

Jesus answered, "I am the way and the truth and the life. No one comes to the Father except through me" (John 14:6).

Then I asked one of my friends if he could show me predictions about Jesus in the Old Testament. He gave me a list of verses, and I read those verses in the Old Testament. Isaiah 53, Psalm 22, Psalm 2 and many others. These verses were about a coming Messiah, Jesus, and his crucifixion.

At this point I had clearly seen that Jesus is the way, the truth, and the life. However, I was afraid of making an eternal mistake. And I found a way . . .

People believe in different religions and all these religions cannot be true. Intelligence is not enough to find God. However, I thought if I pray to God and give this responsibility to God then I should not worry about it. Because I believe that people can make mistakes but God does not. My prayer was similar to this:

God, I want to know you, I want to serve you, I am not seeking the pleasure of paradise, or some religious respect among others, but I only want to know you. I do not want to make a mistake. Please show yourself so that I may know that you are God.

After this prayer, in those weeks, I had a different experience in my life. When I opened the Bible the answers of my questions were right in front of my eyes. I asked for several signs from God to show me that I should follow Jesus. And he always showed those signs.

In 1994, I decided to follow Jesus. Since then, God always increased my faith in Him.

—*Yücel*[14]

ROMAN CATHOLICISM

The Roman Catholic church has always been identified with Christianity, mainly because it upholds the fundamentals of the Christian faith. It teaches the deity of Jesus Christ, the Trinity, the virgin birth, and the bodily resurrection and return of Christ to the earth.

However, most Roman Catholics when asked if they are Christians *will* make a difference between New Testament Christianity and Roman Catholicism. If you ask, "Are you a Christian?" they will normally reply, "I'm a Catholic." They are right to do so, because there are clear and fundamental differences.

With about 1 billion Catholics in the world, it's important that we understand these essential differences.

Background

The Roman Catholic church is said to be the largest organized body of any world religion. According to the *Statistical Yearbook of the Church*, its worldwide membership is around 1.1 million, or approximately one in six of the world's population.

There are two main divisions of traditional Christianity: Roman Catholics and Protestants. The Protestant church is called *protestant* because it "protested" against Catholicism back in the early 1500s. Through study of the Scriptures, a German Catholic monk named Martin Luther found that salvation didn't come through anything he did (his good works), but simply through trusting in the finished work of the cross of Jesus Christ. So he listed the contradictions between what the Scriptures said and what his church taught, and nailed his "95 Theses" to the church door in Wittenberg, Germany. Martin Luther became the first to "protest" what he saw as the errors of the Roman church, and thus he became the father of the Protestant church.

The Catholic church traces its history back to the church of the first century, and maintains that the true Church is built on Peter, whom they believe was the first "pope." However, Peter himself denied this fact, maintaining that Jesus Christ is the Rock and Chief Cornerstone of the Church:

> "Therefore it is also contained in the Scripture, 'Behold, I lay in Zion a chief cornerstone, elect, precious, and he who believes on Him will by no means be put to shame.' Therefore, to you who believe, He is precious; but to those who are disobedient, 'The stone which the builders rejected has become the chief cornerstone'..." (1 Peter 2:6–8)

The Protestant church asserts that Catholicism actually had a later beginning, in the fourth century, when Constantine unified the Roman Empire by merging paganism with Christianity. Declaring himself Vicar of Christ, he elevated "converts" to positions of influence and authority. These professing Christians brought their pagan rites and their gods and goddesses into the church. In time, church councils began to exalt their traditions above Scripture and condemn their opponents, and many devout men were labeled heretics and persecuted for defending the Bible's authority.

By the 12th century the Roman Catholic church had become the world's most powerful institution, using its power to set up and depose kings and queens. It also became the richest institution on earth by taxing people and confiscating property. Through the Crusades and later the Inquisition, the Catholic church put to death Muslims, heretics, and those who rejected papal supremacy.

Scriptures

Roman Catholics use a version of the Bible that includes what's called the Apocrypha, a group of books found in their Old Testament. The Catholic Bible is based on a translation known as the Greek Septuagint, which included these books. Non-Catholics, however, do not accept them as inspired, primarily because the Apocrypha is not part of the official canon of Judaism. The excluded material is a group of fifteen late Jewish books, which were not found in Hebrew versions of the Jewish Scripture.

It is important to realize that the doctrinal differences between Catholics and non-Catholics are not fundamentally caused by the differences in their Scriptures. The problem comes rather with the Roman Catholic church's teachings. For example, it is a puzzle why Roman Catholics bow down to and give homage to statues of "the saints," angels, images of Mary and Jesus, etc. Why do they do such a thing when bowing down to anything is a direct violation of the Ten Commandments—which they officially accept as God's Law?

If you look closely at the Catholic Catechism (the official teachings of the church), you will find that the Second of the Ten Commandments has been completely removed. The Third Commandment then became the Second, the Fourth became the Third, and so on. The Roman Catholic church then took the Tenth Commandment (found in *one* verse and dealing with the *one* subject of covetousness—see Exodus 20:17), broke it in half, and made it into the Ninth and Tenth Commandments. Here are the Ten Commandments as listen on the official Vatican website:

1. I am the LORD your God: you shall not have strange Gods before me.
2. You shall not take the name of the LORD your God in vain.
3. Remember to keep holy the LORD's Day.
4. Honor your father and your mother.
5. You shall not kill.
6. You shall not commit adultery.
7. You shall not steal.

8. You shall not bear false witness against your neighbor.

9. You shall not covet your neighbor's wife.

10. You shall not covet your neighbor's goods.[15]

You won't find a word of the Second Commandment in the Catholic Catechism. This is despite the fact that the Second Commandment is still listed in full in the Roman Catholic Bible.[16] In fact, the Second Commandment against idolatry is cited seven times in the Old Testament and three times in the New Testament (Exodus 20:4; 20:23; 34:17; Leviticus 19:4; 26:1; Deuteronomy 4:23; 5:8; 1 Corinthians 10:7; 10:14; and 1 John 5:21).

While Roman Catholics acknowledge holy Scripture as a source of authority and doctrine, they give equal weight to tradition:

> "...the Church, to whom the transmission and interpretation of Revelation is entrusted, does not derive her certainty about all revealed truths from the holy Scriptures alone. Both Scripture and Tradition must be accepted and honored with equal sentiments of devotion and reverence." (Catechism of the Catholic Church, par. 82)

It is a tragedy that most Roman Catholics give as much credence to the teaching of the church as to the authority of holy Scripture. This is why it is essential to move as quickly as possible from the intellect (arguing *about* Scripture) to the conscience (*using* Scripture, particularly God's Law). It is the Law that "stops every mouth" and brings "the knowledge of sin" (see Romans 3:19,20). Remember, the work of the Law is written on the heart (see Romans 2:15) and will therefore find a place of resonance in the conscience.

Who Is God?

Biblical Christianity and Roman Catholicism share similar beliefs that God is the Creator of all things.

Who Is Jesus?

Biblical Christianity and Roman Catholicism share similar beliefs that Jesus Christ is the Son of God, born of a virgin, who suffered and died for our sins, and rose again on the third day.

Heaven and Hell

According to the Catholic Catechism, upon death each person will begin eternal life. After being judged by Christ each individual will gain "entrance into the happiness of heaven, immediately or after an appropriate purification, or entry into the eternal damnation of hell." Heaven is described as "the state of supreme and definitive happiness [where] those who die in the grace of God and have no need of further purification are gathered around Jesus and Mary, the angels and the saints."

Catholics believe Hell is a place of eternal damnation:

"The teaching of the Church affirms the existence of hell and its eternity. Immediately after death the souls of those who die in a state of mortal sin descend into hell, where they suffer the punishments of hell, 'eternal fire.' The chief punishment of hell is eternal separation from God, in whom alone man can possess the life and happiness for which he was created and for which he longs."[17]

In addition, Catholics believe in a "holding place" called Purgatory, for which there is no biblical basis. It is believed to be an intermediate stage that is used to purify souls that will eventually go to Heaven, but that still have some temporal restitution they must make.

"The Church gives the name *Purgatory* to this final purification of the elect, which is entirely different from the punishment of the damned. The Church formulated her doctrine of faith on Purgatory especially at the Councils of Florence and Trent. The tradition of the Church, by reference to certain texts of Scripture, speaks of a cleansing fire: As for certain lesser faults, we must believe that, before the Final Judgment, there is a purifying fire. He who is truth says that whoever utters blasphemy against the Holy Spirit will be pardoned neither in this age nor in the age to come. From this sentence we understand that certain offenses can be forgiven in this age, but certain others in the age to come."[18]

According to the church, a Catholic can help get someone out of purgatory and into Heaven "by offering prayers in suffrage for them, especially the Eucharistic sacrifice. They also help them by almsgiving, indulgences, and works of penance" (Catechism, par. 211).

> "An indulgence can be obtained through a good deed done, a Mass being offered on behalf of someone, prayer, abstinence, giving to the poor, or some other meritorious act performed in accordance with requirements set by a Pope or bishop having jurisdiction over that individual."[19]

However, according to Scripture, none of our acts are "meritorious"—no amount of good deeds or money can buy eternal salvation: "But Peter said to him, 'Your money perish with you, because you thought that the gift of God could be purchased with money!'" (Acts 8:20).

> "None of them can by any means redeem his brother, nor give to God a ransom for him—for the redemption of their souls is costly..." (Psalm 49:7,8)

The doctrine of Purgatory misleads people into thinking they can somehow be made right with God after this lifetime. Scripture clearly warns us: "It is appointed for men to die once, but after this the judgment" (Hebrews 9:27). There are no second chances.

Sin and Salvation

Understandably, the greatest contention between the Catholic and the Protestant teachings is how a person can be made right with God. The Scriptures clearly teach that the only way we could ever be justified is by His mercy, not by the bribery of good works:

- "For by grace you have been saved through faith, and that not of yourselves; it is the gift of God, not of works, lest anyone should boast" (Ephesians 2:8,9).

- "And if by grace, then it is no longer of works; otherwise grace is no longer grace. But if it is of works, it is no longer grace; otherwise work is no longer work" (Romans 11:6).

- "Not by works of righteousness which we have done, but according to His mercy He saved us…" (Titus 3:5).

The Bible says that eternal life is not something we earn, but is a free gift from God to all who repent and trust the Savior. The Vatican not only denies this doctrine, but condemns it, pronouncing the curse of God upon anyone who believes that eternal life is through "faith alone":

"If any one saith, that by faith alone the impious is justified; in such wise as to mean, that nothing else is required to co-operate in order to the obtaining the grace of Justification…let him be anathema." (Canon 9, Council of Trent)

"If any one saith, that man is truly absolved from his sins and justified…by this faith alone, absolution and justification are effected; let him be anathema." (Canon 14, Council of Trent)

Like the Mormon church and others, the Roman Catholic church teaches that we can earn our salvation, calling Heaven God's "reward for good works":

"We can therefore hope in the glory of heaven promised by God to those who love him and do his will. In every circumstance, each one of us should hope, with the grace of God, to persevere 'to the end' and *to obtain the joy of heaven, as God's eternal reward for the good works* accomplished with the grace of Christ." (Catechism, par. 1821)

"Moved by the Holy Spirit, *we can merit for ourselves and for others all the graces needed to attain eternal life.*" (Catechism, par. 2027)

The Vatican teaches that salvation comes only through the Roman Catholic church, and (because it's works-based), salvation can be lost through sin and is never assured in this life. They believe that the first step in salvation is to be baptized. Tragically, the Roman Catholic church maintains that in baptism (sprinkling) the new birth takes place. Jesus said that each one of us must be born again or we will not enter Heaven (John 3:1–7), but Scripture teaches only what is commonly called "believer's baptism," which occurs after a sinner repents and trusts in Jesus Christ. Because a baby cannot repent of sins committed, he is not saved by baptism—and therefore is not born again.

In Catholicism, baptism erases sins up to that point and merely begins the *process* of salvation, a process that continues throughout life as one participates in the sacraments. The sacrament of penance is required to receive forgiveness of sins committed after baptism. Acts of penance vary but include prayer, saying the rosary, reading Scripture, saying a number of "Our Father" or "Hail Mary" prayers, doing good works, and fasting. In Catholic teaching, the sacraments "are necessary for salvation because they confer sacramental grace, forgiveness of sins, adoption as children of God, conformation to Christ the Lord and membership in the Church. The Holy Spirit heals and transforms those who receive the sacraments" (Catechism, par. 230). God's "grace" that is conferred simply enables believers to perform works that *earn* them the right to Heaven.

Because salvation does not depend on a person's repentance and faith in the saving work of Jesus Christ, according to the Catholic church even those who have never heard of Jesus can be saved—even if they follow of another religion:

> "...thanks to Christ and to his Church, those who through no fault of their own do not know the Gospel of Christ and his Church but sincerely seek God and, moved by grace, try to do his will as it is known through the dictates of conscience can attain eternal salvation." (Catechism, par. 171)

Again, the Bible is clear that forgiveness of sins does not depend on our own efforts, but only on what Christ has accomplished for us on the cross. Yet, like the Catholic church, much of the traditional Protestant church has moved away from the great truth upon which it was once founded. So my purpose isn't necessarily to say that one side is right and the other is wrong. It is simply to say that the gospel is good news for both Catholic and Protestant—eternal life is freely available to all who do what the Scriptures command.

Roman Catholic Beliefs

In rejecting Scripture alone as the sole source of doctrine, the Roman Catholic church has justified several extrabiblical, and unbiblical, teachings. Some of these are discussed below.

Transubstantiation: Transubstantiation is the Roman Catholic doctrine of the Eucharist wafer turning into the *literal* body and blood of Jesus during Mass. The Catechism even specifies when Christ comes into the Eucharist and how long He stays:

> "The Eucharistic presence of Christ begins at the moment of the consecration and endures as long as the Eucharistic species subsist. Christ is present whole and entire in each of the species and whole and entire in each of their parts, in such a way that the breaking of the bread does not divide Christ."[20]

This belief is based on the passage where Jesus said, "Most assuredly, I say to you, unless you eat the flesh of the Son of Man and drink His blood, you have no life in you. Whoever eats My flesh and drinks My blood has eternal life, and I will raise him up at the last day" (John 6:53,54).

Though this might sound like cannibalism, if you read the entire passage in context, the meaning becomes clear. Jesus went on to tell us that He was speaking spiritually: "The words that I speak to you are spirit, and they are life" (John 6:63).

Jesus was explaining that *spiritually*, not physically, all life comes through faith in Him, not through eating His physical body. He is speaking of the new birth (see John 3:1–5) when a sinner believes on Him, and it is then that he tastes of the Lord and Christ dwells in him by faith—"Taste and see that the Lord is good."

This is extremely important because a sinner is saved not by taking the Eucharist, but only by repentance and faith in Christ.

Praying to Saints: The Catholic church believes in praying to those, who, because of their good works, have been exulted to sainthood after their death:

> "The witnesses who have preceded us into the kingdom, especially those whom the Church recognizes as saints, share in the living tradition of prayer by the example of their lives…They contemplate God, praise him and constantly care for those whom they have left on earth. Their intercession is their most exalted service to God's plan. We can and should ask them to intercede for us and for the whole world."[21]

But according to the Bible, *everyone* who is born again by faith alone in Jesus Christ is a saint. For example, in

Romans 1:7, the apostle Paul wrote to all the "saints" (Christians) in Rome, and he called himself a "saint" (Ephesians 3:8). In numerous passages throughout Scripture, *living* Christians are referred to as "saints."[22]

Also, nowhere in Scripture is there any admonition for Christians to pray to someone who has died. Instead, Jesus Himself taught us to pray directly to the Father (Matthew 6:6–9).

Confession to a Priest: The Roman Catholic church says that the priest is the only one who can forgive sins in the name of Christ.[23] However, the good news of the gospel is that *any* sinner can go directly to God and have his sins washed away by the blood of Christ. The Bible tells us that Peter told sinners to go straight to God (not to a man) for forgiveness (see Acts 8:18–22).

Worship of Mary: The Roman Catholic church believes that Mary was "conceived immaculate" (born without original sin) and that she was "kept free from every personal sin her whole life long. She is the one who is 'full of grace' (Luke 1:28), 'the all holy'" (Catechism, par. 95–97). In addition, they believe she remained a virgin after giving birth to Jesus, despite the fact that Scripture says she had other children after she bore Jesus (see Matthew 13:55; Mark 6:3; Galatians 1:19.) Because Mary was supposedly free from sin and its wages (death), they believe that she was taken up to Heaven without experiencing death, in what they call her "Assumption."

The Roman Catholic church refers to Mary as "the Mother of God" and the "Queen of Heaven." Even more alarming, the Catholic Catechism teaches that Mary offers salvation:

"…Taken up to heaven she did not lay aside this saving office but by her manifold intercession continues to bring us the gifts of eternal salvation…Therefore the Blessed Virgin is invoked in the Church under the titles of Advocate, Helper, Benefactress, and Mediatrix." (Catechism, par. 969)

"Mary had only one Son, Jesus, but in him her spiritual motherhood extends to all whom he came to save. Obediently standing at the side of the new Adam, Jesus Christ, the Virgin is the *new Eve*, the true mother of all the living, who with a mother's love cooperates in their birth and their formation in the order of grace. Virgin and Mother, Mary is the figure of the Church, its most perfect realization." (Catechism, par. 100)

However, the Bible says differently. Speaking of Jesus, Scripture says:

- For there is one God and *one Mediator* between God and men, the Man Christ Jesus (1 Timothy 2:5, emphasis added).

- "Nor is there salvation in any other, for there is *no other name* under heaven given among men by which we must be saved" (Acts 4:12, emphasis added).

- "Jesus said to him, "I am the way, the truth, and the life. No one comes to the Father *except through Me*" (John 14:6, emphasis added).

How to Reach a Roman Catholic

Again, the fact that salvation comes by grace through faith alone is wonderful news for both the Roman Catholic and traditional Protestant churches. Eternal life is a free gift of God. Nothing we can do can merit it. All we can do is obey the command to repent and trust the Savior, and the moment we do that we will be born again and be granted the gift of God—eternal life through Jesus Christ our Lord.

Remember, the key to understanding this is a right understanding of our state before God. If we think we are good people, then all we have to do is some good works and that will earn us eternal life. But if we are confronted by God's Law, it shows us that we are desperate criminals in God's sight, and that the only way we could possibly be saved is through His mercy.

So how can we best relate this to a Roman Catholic without insulting and offending him? Let me tell you what I do. When someone says, "I'm a Roman Catholic," I go deaf. Before I understood the use of God's Law to bring to the knowledge of sin, I would panic and think, "Oh dear, now I am going to have to deal with papal infallibility, Mariology, confession to the priest, etc." But now I ignore all that, and simply go straight for the conscience by doing what Jesus did and going through the Ten Commandments.

The Law, in the hand of the Spirit, addresses the conscience and shows the sinner that he's not good, and all the good works in the world cannot and will not bribe a holy God to pervert Eternal Justice.

From Catholicism to Christ

I was born and raised as a Roman Catholic. Out in North Dakota, there is very little gospel witness. I never had any Christian try to witness to me, and as far as I knew, I never had even met a Christian. We were not a religious family, but like most of my friends and the other families I knew, we went to church every Sunday, and Catechism classes on Wednesday nights. I was baptized as an infant into the church, and went through all the rituals throughout my childhood. I would have claimed to believe that Jesus Christ was God manifested in the flesh, and that the Bible was the Word of God. I would have claimed to believe in Heaven and Hell, I believed all that I was taught, intellectually. Nevertheless, I had never understood how sinful I really was in the sight of God, and I never understood the true gospel of Jesus Christ.

When I was around 16 years old, I began to get a little concerned about what would happen to me after I died. From learning about sin in church, and knowing that I was committing these sins every day, I became very concerned. So I began to read the Bible. As I read, and especially through the words of Jesus in the Gospels, I had a growing conviction over my sin. One day I came across Christian television and decided that I would tune in on a regular basis, to look for answers. As I began to listen to a certain preacher, and continued to read the Word of God, I learned that I needed to be "born again" in order to enter the kingdom of God. But one evening, I tuned into a program where men would go out and witness on the streets. They began to go through the Ten Commandments, and I could see myself as guilty of breaking all of them. I saw that I would be guilty on the Day of Judgment according the the Word of God, and would end up in Hell for all of eternity. But I also could see that Hell is exactly what I deserved for sinning against God.

These men went on to explain the good news of the gospel, and I finally understood why Jesus Christ gave His life on the cross and rose again from the dead. I saw my need to turn from my sins once and for all and put my faith in Him. I began to learn about the new birth, about a new heart with new desires that I would receive by God's supernatural work in regeneration.

Full atonement? Could it be? Because of my Roman Catholic background, I thought that my good deeds and participation in the sacraments were the only way I could receive grace. But then I learned that grace comes only through faith, and not in my own good works (Ephesians 2:8,9). I learned that my good works were like filthy rags in God's sight (Isaiah 64:6). Over the passing months the Lord was convicting me of my sin, and by His grace I came to hate the sin that I had always loved, and desired the God that I had rebelled against and ignored my whole life. In the summer of 2004, God brought me to my knees, and saved my soul. I am still amazed in the miracle of the new birth, something that religious works could never bring. Just a short time later, a friend who had moved into the area a few months earlier invited me to a faithful Bible-teaching church. As I grew more and more in the Word of God, I could see that the church I was raised in was not preaching the true gospel of Jesus Christ, and that as His follower, I should leave and go to a church that He wants me to attend and serve in.

I was lost and wasn't seeking God (Romans 3:11), but God sought me out and saved me, and I am forever thankful. I give all the glory to the Great and Sovereign God of the universe.

—*Dean H.*

Witnessing to a Roman Catholic

You: Hello. Nice day.

Paul: Yes, it is.

You: My name is [your name here].

Paul: I'm Paul.

You: Pleased to meet you, Paul.

Paul: Nice to meet you too.

You: Paul, I have an interesting question for you. What do you think happens when someone dies? Is there an afterlife?

Paul: Some people go Hell, some go to Heaven, and some go in-between.

You: Where are you going?

Paul: I think I'm going to Heaven...after a little time in Purgatory.

You: Really? So, do you think that you are basically a good person?

Paul: Most of the time...I'm a Catholic.

[Don't panic. You don't need to get into a conversation about the pope, transubstantiation, etc. In a sense, forget that he said that he is a Catholic, and simply share the gospel with him, emphasizing the new birth and salvation by grace through faith alone.]

You: Have you been born again?

Paul: Probably. When I was confirmed.

You: You would know if you have. When it happens, instead of knowing *about* God, you come to *know* Him personally. Before I was born again I had an intellectual belief in God (I *believed* in Jesus). But the difference between being born again and just believing in Jesus is like the difference between believing in a parachute and actually putting it on. It may not seem important on the flight, but when you jump, you will definitely see the difference. Jesus spoke of the absolute necessity of being born again in John 3:3, where He said, "Unless one is born again, he cannot see the kingdom of God." There's an easy way to find out where you are going after you die. Do you think that you are a good person?

Paul: Yes. I am.

You: Let's go through a few of the Ten Commandments to see how you will do on Judgment Day. How many lies do you think you have told, in your whole life? I mean real lies, not "white" lies.

[Again, make a distinction between what he perceives as permissible lies and deceitfulness.]

Paul: I have told quite a few.

You: Ten? Twenty?

Paul: Probably dozens.

You: What do you call someone who tells lies?

Paul: They are a liar. But I go to confession.

You: Paul, we often think lightly of lying, calling them fibs or "white lies," yet the Scriptures tell us that "lying lips are an abomination to the Lord." That means lies are "extremely detestable" to Him. Have you ever stolen anything, in your whole life?

Paul: Yes. I have.

You: What do you call someone who steals things?

Paul: He is a thief. But like I said, I confessed it to the priest.

You: Confession can't help you.

Paul: It can't?

You: Let me tell you why. Think of a court of law. You are guilty of rape and murder. You may sincerely confess your guilt to the judge, but that's not going to get you off the hook. He won't dismiss your case just because you confess that you committed the crime. He won't even let you go if you say that you are truly sorry and promise never to rape and murder again. You still need to face the punishment for your crimes. Does that make sense?

Paul: Yes, I guess it does.

You: Stay with me. Have you ever used God's name in vain?

Paul: I do it all the time.

You: That's called "blasphemy"—a very serious sin in God's eyes. Jesus said, "Whoever looks at a woman to lust for her has already committed adultery with her in his heart." Have you ever done that?

Paul: All the time.

You: Here's a summary. By your own admission, Paul (I'm not judging you), you are a lying, thieving, blasphemous, adulterer at heart. When you stand before God on Judgment Day, will you be innocent or guilty?

Paul: I will be guilty.

You: Will you go to Heaven or Hell?

Paul: As I said, I will end up in Purgatory.

You: Actually, the Bible doesn't even mention such a place. It says all people will go to either Heaven or Hell. Which would you go to?

Paul: I think I will still go to Heaven.

You: Why?

Paul: Because God is forgiving.

[When a person is under conviction, it is natural for him to try to find a way out. You have to shut every door he tries to open. You can't let him have a false sense of assurance that all is well between him and God.]

You: Do you know what you've done now?

Paul: What?

You: You've broken the Second of the Ten Commandments. It says that you shall not make a false God for yourself. That's when you create a god in your own image, one that you feel comfortable with. That's called "idolatry," and the Bible warns that idolaters will not enter the Kingdom of God. We make up a god in our minds that is all-loving or all-forgiving, when the Bible says that He is also just and holy. We are also told in Scripture that all liars will have their part in the lake of fire. No thief or adulterer will inherit the Kingdom of God. Does it concern you that if you died right now you would go to Hell, forever?

Paul: Yes, it does concern me.

You: Do you know what God did for us, so that we could avoid Hell?

Paul: He died on the cross.

You: Tell me, in you own words what that was about.

Paul: Jesus was giving us an example of how we should be forgiving to our enemies.

You: More than that. It's like this—we broke God's Law (the Ten Commandments) but because Jesus paid our fine on the cross 2,000 years ago in His life's blood, God can now forgive us. He can dismiss your case. He can commute your death sentence. The Bible says, "God demonstrates His own love toward us, in that while we were still sinners, Christ died for us." God proved His great love for you through the cross. Then Jesus rose from the dead, and defeated the power of the grave. If you repent and trust the Savior, God will forgive your sins and grant you everlasting life. Eternal life is a free gift. You can't earn it by doing anything. The Scriptures say, "For by grace you have been saved through faith, and that not of yourselves; it is the gift of God, not of works, lest anyone should boast." Does that make sense to you?

Paul: It sure does. I never understood this before.

You: Paul, if you died right now, where would you go?

Paul: I would go to Hell.

You: So what are you going to do about it?

Paul: I need to repent and trust the Savior.

You: When are you going to do that?

Paul: Next Sunday.

You: You may not be alive next Sunday. Do it today. Go straight to God and confess your sins to Him. You don't need a priest. You can go straight to God Himself. The Bible says, "Whosoever calls upon the name of the Lord shall be saved." Call on Him today. Okay?

Paul: Okay.

You: Thanks for talking to me.

Paul: Thank you.

My wife, Sue, and I were walking around a store when I handed a man a Million Dollar Bill tract. Five minutes later the same man was behind us in the checkout line. He held up the tract and asked, "Are you a Christian?" I said I was. He then said, "I am a Catholic." so I inquired if he had read the message on the back, and to my surprise he said, "I'm going to Hell." When I asked him what he was going to do about it, he replied, "I don't know." So I told him that Jesus took his punishment on the cross, and that he needed to repent and trust the Savior.

He looked blank, so I told him that I would meet him at the front of the store and give him some literature. A moment later I handed him a copy of my book *Hollywood Be Thy Name* and signed it for him. I also gave him a CD of "Hell's Best Kept Secret" and "True and False Conversion." He held up the book and said, "Is this about God?" When I told him it was, he said, "Then this will help me. Thank you," then shook my hand and walked off.

HINDUISM

While you may not have encountered many who follow Hinduism, you've undoubtedly heard of some of its practices. Reincarnation, yoga, meditation, and "being one with God" are all concepts of Hinduism that have influenced our culture. Back in the 1960s, The Beatles helped to popularize Hinduism by promoting Maharishi Mahesh Yogi, a spiritual guru, and through their song "My Sweet Lord." The "Lord" sung about here is not Jesus, but the Hindu deity Krishna. If you've found yourself singing along to this song, you've actually been chanting Hindu prayers!

Background

Hinduism is said to be the oldest and most complex of all religious systems. In reality, nothing is older than Christianity, which began at the moment of creation. It's not easy to give the history of Hinduism, because it doesn't have a defined beginning and it has no specific founder or theology. Hinduism originated in the Indus Valley in modern Pakistan more than three thousand years ago, and now is the world's third largest religion behind Christianity and Islam. It has about 900 million adherents, with a little over a million in the U.S. and the vast majority living in India.

Hindu society is based on a "caste" system, which ranks people by their occupational class:

- Brahmins—priests

- Kshatriyas—soldiers, king-warrior class

- Vaishyas—merchants, farmers, laborers, craftspeople

- Harijahns—the "untouchables"

The higher a person's caste, the more that person is blessed with the benefits and luxuries life has to offer. Although the caste system was outlawed in 1948, it is still important to the Hindu people of India and is still recognized as the proper way to stratify society.

Hinduism actually encompasses a wide variety of religious beliefs, and has been influential in the foundations of other religions, such as Transcendental Meditation, Buddhism, and the New Age Movement. Hindus are tolerant of other religions since they believe that all paths eventually lead to God—because all is God.

Karma

A guiding principle in Hinduism is what is known as "the law of karma"—a law of cause and effect, in which each individual creates his own destiny through his thoughts, words, and deeds. Good actions will lead to good consequences, and bad actions will have the opposite effect.

Often the law of karma isn't accounted for during this life, so it carries over into future lives, trapping individuals in a cycle of reincarnation. Those who have built up a lot of bad karma may be born into a lower caste or even as an animal or insect. It may take many more lifetimes of suffering before they are again reborn as humans. Selfless acts and thoughts as well as devotion to God help one to be reborn at a higher level. This circle of birth, death, and rebirth is known as *samsara*.

Tragically, this belief in karma has great social implications. Because people are considered responsible for their current lot in life, it's believed that those who are suffering or less fortunate are just getting what they deserve based on their karma. Their present suffering helps them to atone for the evil they committed in their previous life. For this reason, charity is almost unheard of.

Scriptures

There is no single source of authority, but Hinduism's vast collection of sacred text includes the following:

- **Vedas:** These four "books of knowledge" are considered the most authoritative. Compiled over about 1,000 years, with no known author, they are a collection of hymns to the various Hindu gods.

- **Upanishads:** The *Upanishads* discuss the idea that behind all gods is the one ultimate reality, Brahman.

- **Ramayana** and **Mahabharata:** These two epics in Hindu literature tell of the mythical incarnations of Vishnu. The *Mahabharata* ("great epic of India") is an approximately 100,000-verse poem, the most famous part of which is the *Bhagavad Gita*. The *Bhagavad Gita* is the most popular of all Hindu texts, and explains how to reach Nirvana.

- **Puranas:** These contain myths, lore, and legends of the Hindu gods.

Who Is God?

In one sense Hinduism is monotheistic, in that it recognizes one supreme deity known as Brahman, or ultimate reality. Brahman is the universe and all it contains; in other words, God is everything and everything is God, a belief known as pantheism. That "everything" includes us: as part of Brahman, that means we are also God. Hinduism has no concept of a personal, knowable God, who is separate from His creation. Brahman alone is all that exists.

In another sense Hinduism is polytheistic, with the worship of multiple deities—though they are all considered manifestations of the one ultimate reality. Brahman is personalized as three separate entities: Brahma (the Creator), Vishnu (the Preserver), and Shiva (the Destroyer). Most Hindus also worship Krishna and Rama, two of Vishnu's ten incarnations, or *avatars*. In addition, forces of nature, animals, and humans can all be deified, giving Hindus a pantheon of 330 million gods and goddesses to worship.

Who Is Jesus?

Hindus are happy to consider Jesus to be one of the many *avatars*, or incarnations, of the impersonal Brahman. But they do not accept Him as the *only* incarnation of God. In no sense is He the unique Son of God, part of the Triune Godhead of the Bible.

Heaven and Hell

Hinduism does not teach a literal Heaven and Hell. The closest they come to the concept of Hell is the suffering endured through numerous lifetimes on earth. The closest thing to Heaven would be to lose their individual identify and be absorbed into the universal oneness.

Sin and Salvation

Hinduism has no concept of sin against a holy God; instead, it teaches that man's greatest problem is his ignorance that he *is* God. In Hindu belief, since Brahman is all that exists, everything else is ultimately an illusion, or *maya*. Our material world, our physical bodies, and our personal existence are all illusions. In essence, then, our ignorance is equivalent to the "Fall" of man: We have forgotten that we are part of Brahman, and have attached ourselves to the desires of the individual self. It is these desires and their consequences that bring suffering, and that subject us to the law of karma.

Though there is no concept of "salvation," the goal of Hindus is to remove the karmic debt and end the cycle of rebirths.

By overcoming the ignorance of their divinity and detaching from self, the individual can be released from personal existence and disappear into the impersonal Brahman. This "liberation" from the wheel of life is called *moksha*. Freed from their physical, personal existence, individuals also become free from all pain and suffering, and become like a drop in the ocean of Brahman.

There are three paths to achieve this liberation:

- **The Way of Works:** Liberation can be obtained through social and religious obligations.

- **The Way of Devotion:** This is the most popular way, and includes acts of worship to any of the numerous gods (*avatars*). Whether in the home or in a temple, worship is primarily done individually rather than as a congregation. Most Hindus worship daily through offerings, rituals, and prayers.

- **The Way of Knowledge:** This way attempts to reach a higher consciousness until one finally realizes his identity with Brahman. This is achieved through study of philosophical writings, yoga, and deep meditation.

How to Reach a Hindu

Once again, here is another religion that is based on good works. As far as the Hindu is concerned, there is no God who warns of Judgment Day, no Heaven, nor is there a Hell. So the same principle of using the Law to bring the knowledge of sin applies to Hindus.

From Hinduism to Christ

I was born in beautiful Trinidad, Caribbean Islands. Hinduism was my religion. I was fascinated by the dances, the rituals involving the different pagan gods, and the movies. I considered myself very religious in spite of a habitual sin that I thought was just a way of life. I was named after one of the Hindu goddesses. My dad practiced Hinduism even though he professed that he was a Christian. My mother was the one who told me about Jesus and that I should always pray to Him, whereas my father taught us that all gods are one.

We celebrated Divali, the "Festival of Lights," where Lakshmi, the goddess of good fortune, is supposed to visit the homes of humans. We also had *pooja* (prayer meetings) very often in our home. I loved the idea that we had a different god for every need and was so very caught up with what I could become after I died because reincarnation was real to me.

I became obsessed with Indian dancing and around the age of 9 performed in the Hindu Temples for all the religious activities to the pagan gods. My dream was to go to

India, become a classical Indian dancer, and live the Hindu life.

After graduating from high school, my religious life continued. I fasted and lighted *deyas* (clay pot with oil) because I believed that the gods would answer my prayers. I also frequently visited a Hindu Pundit who read my future. I would dream of the pagan gods and believed that was a good thing; when I dreamt of the goddess Kali, I knew something bad was going to happen. I was told by the Pundit that the people I was living with were trying to do bad things to me. I had to purchase a fig tree, light *deyas* every night, do an offering, and then pour milk over the tree for two weeks. Every time I went back to him it cost $75. Nothing happened and he kept telling me that they cast spells on me, so he required that I do some other things but I got wise to him and never went back.

One of my coworkers, whose husband was a pastor, would tell me that they were praying for me. I thought, "What weird people...I am good. Why did they think I needed prayer?" A supervisor said to me one day, "Ambica, I just can't believe that Jesus would die for me," and what stayed with me were the tears in her eyes. She was really in love with Jesus; she really believed that He did this for her.

I started going to a Baptist church. On New Years Eve I heard, "Repent of your sins" and I realized that earlier I kept thinking I needed someone like Jesus to forgive my sins. Going to hell was not even on my mind because I always thought that heaven and hell were right where we were.

When I got home, I knew without a doubt that something happened. I came to know the real Jesus. I came to understand God the Father, God the Son, and God the Holy Spirit are not three individuals who are separated but the Godhead who is a triune God. Hinduism has many deities, and they also worship the trees, animals, spirits, and other things. Hinduism is a way of life, bound up with its own traditions and its own beliefs.

My Lord made me whole; He removed religion from my life and replaced it with a relationship with Him. Jesus opened my eyes to see that Hinduism is a cult. It is a lie that we can be "born-again Christians" and still be a Hindu, Muslim, or any other religion. There is only one God and His name is not Ram, Shiva, Lakshman, Ganesh, or Allah. He is God, Creator of all heaven and earth. Jesus Christ is God. Without His forgiveness, no one can enter the Kingdom of God.

— *Ambica C.*

Witnessing to a Hindu

You: Hi. How are you doing? My name is [your name here].

Ravish: Very well, thank you, sir. I'm Ravish.

You: Good to meet you, Ravish. What does your name mean?

Ravish: It means "sun ray" or "beam of light."

You: Interesting. I have a question for you, Ravish. What do you think happens after someone dies?

Ravish: I believe in reincarnation. We come back as something else.

You: You mean another person?

Ravish: Yes. Or an animal. It depends on how you live your life. If you are a good person, you come back as something good.

You: So, who's in charge of giving out the new bodies?

Ravish: It has to do with karma. If you do good things, it will come back to you in this life or the next. Things like compassion, love, non-violence, truth, and forgiveness are divine characteristics that will accumulate good karma. Lust, anger, greed, arrogance, pride, and hypocrisy are negative characteristics.

You: Do you believe in Heaven?

Ravish: No. Not really. Not a physical place.

You: What do you think you did in your last life to merit coming back in this one as a man?

Ravish: I don't know.

You: How are you doing morally in this life?

Ravish: I'm doing very well, sir.

You: Ravish, let's see if you will come back as a prince or as a cockroach. Do you think you are a good person?

Ravish: Yes. I believe that I'm a very good person.

You: How many lies do you think you have told, in your whole life? I don't mean "white" lies. I mean real lies.

Ravish: One or two. Maybe three or four.

You: So, what do you call someone who tells lies?

Ravish: They are called liars. But everyone tells lies.

You: Have you ever stolen anything, in your whole life, even if it was small?

Ravish: Yes. Little things. When I was a small boy.

You: What do you call someone who steals things?

Ravish: They are called a thief.

You: Have you ever used God's name in vain?

[You will more than likely find that American culture—particularly Hollywood—has made biblical blasphemy universal.]

Ravish: Yes, sir, I have.

You: God gave you your eyes to see the beauty of His creation, and ears to listen to good music. He gave you taste buds to enjoy all the wonderful foods He has made. He lavished His goodness upon you, and yet you have taken His holy name and used it as a cuss word to express disgust.

That's a very serious crime in His eyes—it's called "blasphemy."

Ravish: Yes, sir. I know that it's wrong.

You: Jesus said, "Whoever looks upon a woman with lust has already committed adultery with her in his heart." Have you ever looked at a woman with lust?

Ravish: Yes, I have done that, very many times.

You: Ravish, you've admitted to me (and I'm not judging you) that you are a liar, a thief, a blasphemer, and an adulterer at heart; and you have to face God on Judgment Day whether you believe He is personal or not. The Bible says that all liars will have their part in the lake of fire. They will end up in a place called "Hell." Also, no thief, blasphemer, or adulterer will enter Heaven.

Ravish: I believe that Hell is here on earth. Actually, I believe in karma.

You: If I stood in front of a judge and said, "Judge, I know that I am guilty of murder, but I don't believe in the electric chair," my unbelief doesn't change anything. And there is no reincarnation. The Bible says, "It is appointed to man once to die, but after this, the judgment." So, does it concern you that if you died right now and God gave you justice, you would end up in Hell forever?

Ravish: Yes, it certainly does.

You: Do you know what God did, so that we wouldn't have to go to Hell?

Ravish: No, I don't know what He did.

You: God became a morally perfect human being and gave His life as a sacrifice for the sin of the world. We broke God's Law (the Ten Commandments) but because Jesus paid our fine on the cross 2,000 years ago, God can dismiss our case. He can forgive us, and commute our death sentence. He can let us live.

The Bible says, "God demonstrates His own love toward us, in that while we were still sinners, Christ died for us." God proved His great love for you through the cross. Then Jesus rose from the dead, and defeated the power of the grave. Ravish, if you repent and trust the Savior, God will forgive your sins and grant you everlasting life. Does that make sense?

Ravish: Yes, it does.

You: Ravish, where would you go, according to the Bible, if your heart gave out and you died right now?

Ravish: I guess I would go to Hell.

You: You are right. All liars will have their part in the lake of fire. No thief, blasphemer, or adulterer will inherit the Kingdom of God. What are you going to do about it?

Ravish: I will ask God to forgive my sins.

You: That's right. Repent, and trust in Jesus. When are you going to do that?

Ravish: I have been doing it while we have been speaking.

You: Ravish, thank you for listening to me. I have a booklet I would like to give you called "Save Yourself Some Pain." It will help you grow as a Christian.

BUDDHISM

With about 375 million adherents, Buddhism is the fourth-largest religion in the world behind Christianity, Islam, and Hinduism. There are only about 1.5 million Buddhists living in the U.S., so their beliefs may not be very familiar to you.

It is the dominant religion of the Far East and is becoming increasingly popular in the West, especially among movie stars. Many of us associate Buddhism with celebrities like Richard Gere, monks dressed in orange, and, of course, the most famous of all Buddhists, the Dalai Lama.

Buddhism appeals to many because it promotes non-violence and tolerance, and offers a moral life of peace, tranquility, and enlightenment—all without any accountability or obligation to a God. It may sound odd, but God has as much place in Buddhism as in atheism—yet both belief systems are considered religions. The Buddhist's view of God is explained in *A Basic Buddhism Guide:*

> There is no almighty God in Buddhism. There is no one to hand out rewards or punishments on a supposed Judgment Day. Buddhism is strictly not a religion *in the context of being a faith and worship owing allegiance to a supernatural being.*[24]

Over its long history Buddhism has developed into a wide variety of forms, ranging from an emphasis on religious rituals and worship of deities to a complete rejection of both rituals and deities in favor of pure meditation. But all share in common a great respect for the teachings of the Buddha, "The Enlightened One."

Background

Buddhism was founded around the 5th century B.C. by an Indian prince named Siddhartha Gautama. According to tradition, the young prince lived an affluent and sheltered life until a journey during which he saw an old man, a sick

man, a poor man, and a corpse. What he observed was that nothing lasted—people desired to hold on to life, health, possessions, and each other. But all these things pass away, which causes suffering.

Troubled by these scenes of human pain and suffering, on his 29th birthday Gautama left his wife and infant son on a search for truth and the meaning of life. After wandering for six years, and experimenting with yoga, asceticism, and near starvation, Gautama sat beneath a tree and vowed not to move until he had attained enlightenment.

Days later, the 35-year-old prince felt he attained understanding and arose as the Buddha—the "Enlightened One." He spent the remaining 45 years of his life teaching the path to liberation from suffering (the *dharma*) and establishing a community of monks (the *sangha*).

In the 2,500 years since the Buddha's enlightenment, Buddhism has spread over many countries, split into numerous sects, and adopted a wide variety of beliefs, practices, rituals and customs. It has evolved into three main philosophies, or schools:

- **Theravada** (the "Doctrine of the Elders") represents approximately 38% of the Buddhist population. Theravada is the closest to the original atheistic philosophy.

- **Mahayana** (the "Greater Vehicle") represents approximately 56% of Buddhists. Over the years, Mahayana has accommodated many different Asian beliefs and now worships Buddha as a god.

- **Vajrayana** (also known as Lamaism or Tantrism) represents the remaining 6% of Buddhists. Vajrayana has added elements of shamanism and the occult.

Some groups may involve more animistic superstitions than others. Many participate in idol worship, the veneration of the spirits of dead ancestors, and ceremonial rituals to appease evil spirits. The beliefs, practices, rites and ceremonies, customs and habits of Buddhists can vary in different countries, making them especially difficult to define. The following is just a sampling of some of their views on the important topics of God, the afterlife, and salvation.

Scriptures

There are a large number of religious texts and scriptures in Buddhism. The *Sutras* are considered to be the actual sayings of Buddha. The *Tripitaka* is one of the earliest compilations of Buddhist teachings. Over the years, many new observations were added until today it consists of up to 50 volumes—and it's more than 10 times larger than the Bible. The collection is also known as the Pali Canon and is considered sacred by some.

Other texts consist of observations on the Sutras, compilations of quotes, histories, grammars, etc.

Who Is God?

One doctrine agreed upon by all branches of modern Buddhism is that "This world is not created and ruled by a God."[25] The idea of a personal, loving Creator who interacts with people is foreign to Buddhists. It is thought that Siddhartha Gautama rejected theistic beliefs because he had difficulty reconciling the reality of suffering, judgment, and evil with the existence of a good and holy God.

Although Buddhism does not concern itself with God and the afterlife, some say that Buddha (Gautama) did not rule out the existence of a God or gods altogether. So as

Buddhism grew and spread, local deities and religious practices were included in it. Today, Tibetan Buddhists believe
in a large number of "divine beings."

Gautama never taught that he was a god or that he
should be worshiped as a god, but the Mahayana sect believes Buddha became a *Bodhisattva*, a savior-like god, and
can be called upon for help. The Mahayana believe numerous celestial Buddhas and Bodhisattvas occupy the universe
as gods and goddesses that assist and inspire the Buddhist
practitioner, while the Theravada sect of Buddhism does
not believe in the existence of deities.

Who Is Jesus?

Most Buddhists would probably consider Jesus to be an
Enlightened Master, though definitely not the Son of God.
The Dalai Lama believes that Jesus is "a fully enlightened
being." In an article in *Christianity Today*, the interviewer
challenged the Dalai Lama with this thought:

> "If Jesus is fully enlightened, wouldn't he be teaching
> the truth about himself? Therefore, if he is teaching
> the truth, then he is the Son of God, and there is a
> God, and Jesus is the Savior. If he is fully enlightened,
> he should teach the truth. If he is not teaching the
> truth, he is not that enlightened."[26]

The Dalai Lama stated that Jesus had lived previous lives
and that His purpose was to teach a message of tolerance
and compassion, to help us become better human beings.

Heaven and Hell

Buddhism does not teach eternal life spent in either a Heaven or Hell after death. They may consider it "Hell" to have to endure the untold sufferings of many lifetimes on earth, but they don't believe in any place of eternal punishment. There also is no place of eternal reward in Heaven. Instead, their goal in life is to reach Nirvana, or Enlightenment—a state of mind that is free from desire.

Sin and Salvation

The idea of original sin, or of sin at all, has no place in Buddhism, so there is no need for salvation from sin and its consequences. In fact, Buddhists believe that people do not have individual souls. Instead, they are composed of five elements (physical form, feelings, ideations, mental developments and awareness) that combine to form a human being at the time of birth. Although there is no eternal soul to continue on after death, Buddhism still believes in karma and reincarnation (rebirth). Their view differs from the Hindu view, however.

In Hinduism, the same individual is reincarnated into another body through numerous lives, as he continually tries to work out his karma. In Buddhism, a person who dies is reborn as someone else. Still, because Buddhists believe in karma, they contend that the person's achievements in life will continue on into their next bodily form. The way they explain it is that "the consciousness of a person remains even after he is no more. It even manifests in his future life." So the person continues, but there is no soul. As one Buddhist website admits, "One finds a little contradiction here."[27]

Because karma, the Buddhist law of moral cause and effect, is completely rigid and impersonal, life for a Buddhist is very oppressive. Under karma, there can be no appeal, no mercy, and no escape except through unceasing effort at self-perfection. Through numerous lifetimes, Buddhists endure an endless cycle of continuous suffering, and their goal is to break out of this cycle by finally extinguishing the flame of life and entering a permanent state of pure nonexistence (Nirvana). The ultimate goal of the Buddhist is not life, but death (extinction) by releasing their attachment to desire and the self. The reward for all their ceaseless labor is therefore to cease to exist. In this way they hope to achieve liberation and freedom ("salvation") from suffering.

Buddhist Customs

The essential elements of the Buddhist belief system are summarized in the Four Noble Truths, the Noble Eightfold Path, and several additional key doctrines.

The Four Noble Truths affirm that:

1. Life is full of suffering (*dukkha*).

2. Suffering is caused by craving (*samudaya*).

3. Suffering will cease only when craving ceases (*nirodha*).

4. Suffering can be eliminated by following the Noble Eightfold Path.

The Noble Eightfold Path supposedly is the way to the cessation of suffering. It includes the following:

1. Right Understanding—Understanding reality as it is, not just as it appears to be.

2. Right Thought—Change in the pattern of thinking.

3. Right Speech—One speaks in a non-hurtful, not exaggerated, truthful way.

4. Right Action—Wholesome action, avoiding action that would do harm.

5. Right Livelihood—One's way of livelihood does not harm in any way oneself or others, directly or indirectly.

6. Right Effort—One makes an effort to improve.

7. Right Mindfulness—Mental ability to see things for what they are with clear consciousness.

8. Right Concentration—Being aware of the present reality within oneself, without any craving or aversion (involves deep meditation).

The Noble Eightfold Path is seen as a practical guideline for ethical and mental development to free the individual from "attachments and delusions" (things that cause suffering). Buddhists believe that following it will lead to understanding the truth about all things. They emphasize the practical aspect, because it is only through practice that they can hope to attain a higher level of existence and finally reach Nirvana. The eight aspects of the path are not a sequence of steps, but are attitudes and actions that can be developed simultaneously.

The Five Precepts are the basis of Buddhist morality. They are not given in the form of commands such as "Thou shalt not...," but are training rules in order to live a better life in which one is happy, without worries, and can meditate well. The Five Precepts, in general, consist of five abstentions:

1. Abstain from harming living beings (non-violence toward sentient life forms). This includes human beings, animals and insects. However, Buddhists can eat meat, if the being has not been killed for them specifically.

2. Abstain from stealing, which means not taking what is not given.

3. Abstain from sexual misconduct. This includes being unfaithful to one's partner, involvement with prostitution or pornography, immoral thoughts, etc.

4. Abstain from false speech, which includes lying, gossiping, etc. This means speaking the truth always.

5. Abstain from intoxicating drinks and drugs (which lead to loss of mindfulness), except those taken for medicinal purposes.[28]

How to Reach a Buddhist

It's clear from the teachings of Buddhism that this is another works-righteousness religion, with a fear that if righteousness isn't attained, there with be another rebirth into this world of suffering.

Hollywood has made reincarnation look to many like an intriguing alternative to Heaven. So many latch onto the belief that they may have lived another life in the past and will return after death in another life. But a little probing shows that they haven't given much thought about their belief: Who is in charge of giving out bodies? What is God's (or whoever's in charge) criteria for doing so? If they are hoping to come back as royalty or a great stallion, what do they have to do in this life to merit such a reward? Or what does one have to do or be to end up coming back as a cockroach? What were they in past lives, and what did they do to merit the life they have now? Asking some of these questions may help them see that their belief is illogical, and has no proof.

Then share with them the Good News, that if they want to go where there is no more suffering, there's only one Way for that to happen—and it's a belief that can be backed up by verifiable proof.

As in other religions, Buddhism uses some of the same words as Christianity, but with entirely different meanings. For example, to avoid confusion, don't tell a Buddhist that he must be "born again." Since the Buddhist's goal is to *avoid* being reborn, that phrase indicates failure and gives a negative view of what becoming a Christian means. Instead, explain to him that he can be born as a new person spiritually and be saved eternally.

From Buddhism to Christ

I am a 34-year-old, born-again Christian who loves God and hates sin. As a Chinese growing up in Taiwan, I was led to believe in Buddhism by my father without examining the truth of it for myself. I just blindly went along with what my father and the Chinese society believed. I worshipped the Buddha, the mother god Guanyin, thousand-armed "*pooza*" gods, and other ugly gods with long ears and pimpled heads. Buddhism was never able to answer for me questions such as the origin and creation of the universe, the purpose of man's existence, and the purpose of my life.

After being exposed to Christianity at the age of 23, I went to the national central library in Taiwan (the biggest in Taiwan) and found out that Buddha never claimed to be a god nor did he want to be worshipped as a god. That all came from people's actions after his death. The name Buddha means "the enlightened one." However, he died at the age of 80, in 543 B.C., after eating poisoned pork and suffering severe pain. Obviously, to me this alone proved that he is not the all-knowing God of the universe, and that he is not "enlightened" and all-knowing enough to prevent his own painful death.

Today the body of Buddha lies in a grave in Kusinara, at the foot of the Himalaya Mountains. But the body of Jesus has resurrected from the dead, proving Jesus has victory over sin and death and is now able to grant us eternal life if we repent of our sins and trust in Him as Lord and Savior.

The facts of life after death still remain an unsolved mystery in Buddhism. So the logical conclusion is: since Buddha can't even resurrect his own dead body after death, then how can he resurrect mine and grant me eternal life?

Buddhists hope to enter into the state of Nirvana through meditation and self-denial. The term Nirvana means "the blowing out" of existence, unlike the Christian concept of heaven. A supposed eternal state of the end of human suffering and being blended into the universe. However, common sense tells me that I don't want to die and be blended into the universe like an ant being trampled by death and blended into mud. I rather choose to extend my life through the free gift of eternal life from God! I'd rather be welcomed into heaven than blended into mud and death. My soul, my conscience, and common sense all scream out at me, telling me to choose life instead of "the blowing out" of existence.

Then about two years ago, after hearing from evangelist Ray Comfort of the true Gospel and the use of God's moral law in converting the soul (Psalm 19:7; Romans 7:7), I realized that I was a sinner who had transgressed nearly all of the Ten Commandments. My wife and I repented of all of the sins listed in the Ten Commandments, accepted Jesus as Lord and Savior, and got truly born again. I realized that the suffering of mankind was a direct result of the sin problem of man. It's obvious that the Buddhist's way of meditation isn't the medication needed for the disease of sin. The medication needed is the Gospel of Jesus Christ! My wife

> and I now have a strong desire for continued holiness and we use God's moral law in evangelism. All glory to Jesus and many thanks to Ray Comfort.
> —*Johnson M.*

Witnessing to a Buddhist

You: Hi. How are you doing? My name is [your name here].

Dasbala: Good. I'm Dasbala.

You: Good to meet you, Dasbala. I have a question for you. What do you think happens after someone dies?

Dasbala: I think that they are reborn as someone else.

You: Do you believe in God?

Dasbala: I'm a Buddhist. Most Buddhists don't believe in a personal God or any divine being. Generally, we don't worship anything.

You: Are you an atheist?

Dasbala: Oh, no. I do believe in some sort of life force that created everything.

You: So what's the point of being a Buddhist?

Dasbala: The goal is to reach the state of Nirvana. This word means "to extinguish" or "to blow out of existence." It means to get rid of the ego or self.

You: Do you believe in a place called Heaven?

Dasbala: No, Nirvana is very different from the Christian concept of Heaven. What exactly this is, Buddha never really put into words, but we know that it is a release from suffering, from desire, and from the finite state of self. Buddha himself was not certain what lay beyond death. He didn't leave any clear teaching on the afterlife.

You: So you don't have any hope of everlasting life?

Dasbala: No. Not really. I know a little bit about Christianity, and what we have in Buddhism is different in that it doesn't offer any form of redemption, or forgiveness. There's no hope of a Heaven, or a final Day of Judgment. Buddhism is really a moral philosophy.

You: So how are you doing morally?

Dasbala: I'm doing okay.

You: Dasbala, let's suppose that there is a Heaven, just for a moment. Do you think you are good enough to go there? Are you a good person?

Dasbala: Yes. I believe that I'm a good person.

You: How many lies do you think you have told, in your whole life? I don't mean "white" lies. I mean real lies.

Dasbala: Perhaps six.

You: Six. So, what do you call someone who tells lies?

Dasbala: They are human beings, with weaknesses ... everyone tells lies.

You: Yes. But what would you call *me* if I told lies?

Dasbala: A liar.

You: Have you ever stolen anything, in your whole life, even if it was small?

Dasbala: Yes, I have. But they were only little things, and it was in the past—when I was younger.

You: What do you call someone who steals things?

Dasbala: A thief.

You: I know that you don't believe in a personal God, but have you ever used His name in vain?

Dasbala: Yes, I have. Once or twice.

You: God gave you eyes to see the beauty of this incredible creation, and ears to listen to good music. He gave you taste buds to enjoy all the wonderful foods. He lavished His kindness upon you, and then you have taken His holy name and used it as a cuss word to express disgust. That's a very serious crime in His eyes—it's called "blasphemy."

Dasbala: I know it's wrong to do that.

You: Jesus said, "Whoever looks upon a woman with lust has already committed adultery with her in his heart." Have you ever looked at a woman with lust?

Dasbala: Yes, I have, many times.

You: Dasbala, you've admitted that (and I'm not judging you) you are a liar, a thief, a blasphemer, and an adulterer at heart; and you have to face God on Judgment Day whether you believe in Him or not. The Bible says that all liars will have their part in the lake of fire, and that no thief, blasphemer, or adulterer will enter Heaven.

Dasbala: I don't believe that there is a place called Hell. Hell is on earth. It's karma.

You: If I stood in front of a judge and said, "Judge, I know that I am guilty of murder, but I don't believe in the electric chair," it's not going to change anything. My unbelief doesn't change reality. So, does it concern you that if you died right now and God gave you justice, you would end up in Hell forever?

Dasbala: Yes, I suppose it does.

You: Do you know what God did for us, so that we could avoid Hell?

Dasbala: I know that He sent His Son to die on the cross.

You: That's right. God became a morally perfect human being, Jesus of Nazareth, and gave His life as a sacrifice for the sin of the world. We broke God's Law (the Ten Commandments) but because Jesus paid our fine on the cross 2,000 years ago, God can dismiss our case. He can commute our death sentence. The Bible says, "God demonstrates His own love toward us, in that while we were still sinners, Christ died for us." God proved His great love for you through the cross. Then Jesus rose from the dead, and defeated the power of the grave. Dasbala, if you repent and trust the Savior, God will forgive your sins and grant you everlasting life. Does that make sense?

Dasbala: Yes. I never really understood that before.

You: So, Dasbala, where would you go, according to the Bible, if you died right now?

Dasbala: I think I would go to Hell.

You: What are you going to do about it?

Dasbala: I will definitely think about what you have said.

You: Please do more than think about it. Hell is very real. You must repent and trust the Savior, Jesus Christ.

Dasbala: Yes, you are right.

You: When are you going to do that?

Dasbala: I would like to do that now.

You: Okay. You pray and ask God to forgive your sins, and put your trust in Jesus, and then I will pray for you.

Dasbala: Okay. "Oh, God. I am sinful. I have done these things. Please forgive me for them. I hope you will do that. I trust Jesus to help me from now on and to keep me clean. Thank you. Amen."

You: "Father, may this be the day of salvation for Dasbala. May this day be the day he is forgiven and cleansed of all sin. Please raise him up as a testimony to your incredible salvation. Bless him and his family, and keep them in health. In Jesus' name I pray. Amen." Give me a hug, Dasbala. I have a booklet for you called "Save Yourself Some Pain." It will help you to grow as a Christian.

ATHEISM

One dictionary definition of the word "religion" is: "A cause, principle, or activity pursued with zeal or conscientious devotion." That rightly describes the ardent atheist's cause. Despite protests to the contrary by its faithful adherents, atheism is a form of religion. In 1961, the Supreme Court described "secular humanism" as a religion and said that a religion need not be based on a belief in the existence of a supreme being.

What are known as the "new atheists" have an *unwavering* faith that there is no evidence for the existence of God, and their numbers are quickly growing in the United States and Europe. Some even meet regularly for fellowship, where among other things they talk about their belief that God doesn't exist. Though they consider themselves intellectual, the Bible calls the professing atheist a "fool" (see Psalm 14:1). This is because he *knows* intuitively that God exists. He *suppresses* the truth in willful ignorance:

"But God shows his anger from Heaven against all sinful, wicked people who suppress the truth by their wickedness. They know the truth about God because He has made it obvious to them. For ever since the world was created, people have seen the earth and sky. Through everything God made, they can clearly see His invisible qualities—His eternal power and divine nature. So they have no excuse for not knowing God. Yes, they knew God, but they wouldn't worship Him as God or even give Him thanks. And they began to think up foolish ideas of what God was like. As a result, their minds became dark and confused. Claiming to be wise, they instead became utter fools." (Romans 1:18–22, New Living Translation)

The Scriptures tell us that God has given "light" to every man (see John 1:9). This is evident in the fact that only 2 percent of the world's 6.5 billion inhabitants claim to not believe in God. The problem with the atheist is that he has switched the light off. Our job (with the help of God) is to turn it back on, which we'll look at later.

To consider the "religious beliefs" of the average atheist, I've taken the liberty to ask for input from the atheists who frequent my daily blog, "Atheist Central."[29] Their beliefs are presented differently than in the other religions, in that I'm letting the atheists speak for themselves about what they believe. I thought it might be helpful for you to hear the very arguments that atheists often use, in case you encounter them in witnessing.

Interspersed with their beliefs, I have included some thoughts (shown in brackets) on how to counter their thinking.

Lunch with an Atheist

An atheist who is the boss of a "backyard" skeptics club asked me to have lunch with him. Bruce was a nice man, so we made a date to eat together. After I said grace, we chatted for about 40 minutes and then went back to our ministry to answer some questions his fellow skeptics had formulated. As we sat down, he boldly put a small recording device into my top pocket. I felt as though I was being set up, but decided to see where he was leading me.

They were the usual questions skeptics ask. Here are a few that I recall: "Why do you reject all the evidence of evolution given by paleontologists?" I told him that I was a skeptic by nature, and that evidence for evolution given by paleontologists should be viewed with great skepticism, because they had big motives for lying. If a paleontologist comes up with any sort of evidence, he could find his face on the cover of *National Geographic*, with worldwide TV interviews, a book deal, and big honorariums for speaking engagements. So the modern paleontologist has a huge incentive for twisting the truth, just a little. (There is also all the evidence *against* evolution given by paleontologists, which *he* is rejecting, but we didn't get into that.)

Next question: "Why doesn't God show Himself by doing a little miracle, like simply moving a glass of water on the desk in front us?" I reminded him that over lunch he mocked the miracle of God causing the sun to stand still for Joshua. That was significantly bigger and better than moving a glass. Besides, if he wanted an audience with the Queen of England, she doesn't come on his terms, he comes on hers. He mumbled, "Good analogy."

He then asked me why there were so many religions. I told him that man messes up everything to which he puts his hand, *especially* religion, and that I hate religion. I explained that the difference between being a Christian and being "religious" is something called "works righteousness." Religious people think that they can earn (or bribe) their way to Heaven by doing things—fasting, praying, facing Mecca, good works, etc.—when eternal life is a free gift of God. It cannot be earned. I said that I would rather be called "stumpy" than "religious." Religion has caused untold wars and misery throughout history, it's the opiate of the masses, and I don't run around in a white robe sprinkling water on people.

As I was answering his questions I was thinking that things weren't going the way my friend expected. I became convinced that he wouldn't post the interview on the skeptics' website. It wasn't good for his cause.

The next time I saw Bruce, my thoughts were confirmed. He said that he had decided not to post it because I had mentioned the Bible too many times. If I recall correctly, I may have referred to it two or three times. Besides, he was in the broadcasting business, so I guess he must have forgotten about something called "editing."

The incident confirmed what I had believed all along. The skeptic isn't interested in truth. He only wants to confirm his presuppositions. That's why they have their club—to build up each other in their faith (beliefs). How true that "men loved darkness rather than light, because their deeds were evil. For everyone practicing evil hates the light and does not come to the light, lest his deeds should be exposed." Oops. I quoted the Bible.

Who Is God?

"All atheists disbelieve in all gods."

"Atheists believe no one has yet provided enough evidence to warrant a belief in god(s) or in the Christian context, God."[30]

"There is no reason to believe that a supernatural intelligent creator exists."

[There are *billions* of reasons to believe in a supernatural intelligent Creator. From the order of DNA, to every atom, to the amazingly designed tiny fleas, to the massive elephants, to the sun and its circuit, to the millions of stars and the entire universe, there is incredible order. If you were walking along a beach and saw words written in the sand that said, "Johnny, make sure you come home at 5:00 p.m. for dinner. See you then. I love you. Mom xxxx," could you ever believe that the order of the words happened by a random process—an accident? Could you conclude that perhaps the incoming waves left the words in the sand? Only a fool would think so. Their very order, information content, and constructed logic tell you that the message was written by an intelligent mind.]

"No such thing. There's no one who had a hand in creating the Universe, us, and who cares what we do with our lives. Just as real as Santa Claus and Zeus."

"Gods are what people think up before they understand the world around them. Gods die when answers to these mysteries are discovered and the old ones finally stop teaching the kids the lie."

"I don't believe that such a being exists. While I can't—and don't—rule out the possibility, I can say that postulating a God or gods doesn't usefully explain any observed phenomenon, and so I treat the idea in much the same way that I treat ghosts and fairies. Although, like ghosts and fairies, I can't rule them out, I think it's insensible to believe in them without compelling evidence first. After reading widely, I haven't found Zeus or Apollo or Tûmatauenga or Shiva or Molech convincing, and I don't find any compelling evidence for YHWH (the Christian God) either..."

[This is a popular philosophy parroted by contemporary atheists, and for those simple folk who don't see creation as compelling, axiomatic evidence for a Creator, it seems convincing enough. This is because it paints theists as naive simpletons, and atheists as practical and thinking persons, when the opposite is the case.]

"The closer we look at reality, the less need there is to postulate any being to explain nature. I am personally an 'agnostic atheist,' meaning that I do not and cannot rule out the possibility of a creator underlying the laws of nature themselves, but I find the likelihood of the existence of any such being to be astronomically small."

"There is none. That is to say, there was no 'intelligence' that created the universe, no source of good and evil beyond humanity itself, no supernatural all-powerful force with a will."

"An idea that is meant to be mainly a safety blanket, a guarantee of our 'specialness,' a way to cope with the unknown. That is not to say that God exists. I don't think he does in any tangible or meaningful sense, other than inside the collective imaginations of human beings of one creed or another. Which, in short, doesn't affect reality at all."

"One might suppose that at least atheists would have a uniform opinion on the God (to wit: there isn't One). The trouble is, since there's no authority to regulate who can call himself an atheist, that can excommunicate atheists, you get cases like the recent Pew Forum poll that found that 6% of self-described atheists believe in a personal God, and another 12% believe in an impersonal God . . . If there's one thing that I would expect to unite atheists, it's an attitude that it's not up to them to prove that there is no God. They don't see atheism as comparable to believing there is no gold in China; they see it more as believing that there are no dragons in China, and would insist that the burden of proof is on you to actually provide evidence for either Chinese dragons or God, not on them to check under every sofa cushion and rock in China to make sure that no dragon is hiding there."

[The "burden of proof" is a favorite defense among modern atheists. It means that he can sit back as judge, and require the Christian to provide "credible" evidence. If the Christian doesn't provide proof, he feels completely exonerated in his belief that God doesn't exist. Yet, the judge is no judge at all. He's a devious criminal demanding "evidence" when creation is staring him in the face.]

"There probably aren't any gods or deities."

Who Is Jesus?

"Whether Jesus existed or not we may never know. I have mixed opinions on the subject. If he did exist then I think he was probably a very good teacher, who had interesting philosophies. If he claimed to be the Son of God then I would think he was mentally unstable, and probably got a load of followers the same way modern day 'messiahs' like Michael Travesser[31] do."

"Atheism, by definition, lacks an opinion on the subject of Jesus other than rejecting the notion that he is a god."

"A radical Jewish rabbi that may or may not have lived around 2,000 years ago. If he did live, he was human, probably had a wife and children. His influence was great, and he had a few followers at first. After his death, his fellowship grew, and his followers eventually couldn't fathom that a man was responsible for their teachings and they deified him by removing passages from their texts that retained his humanity, and emphasizing passages that deified him."

"Mostly mythological."

"I believe someone existed at some point with that name, was Jewish, and had a following. Whether he did anything in the New Testament is a different thing."

[Most people have no idea that the entire Bible is about one person—Jesus of Nazareth. It speaks of Him from the Book of Genesis to the Book of Revelation. It tells us that He created all things, including the eyes you are using to see these words, the lungs that are breathing in the oxygen He created, to feed the brain that He made so you can process them (see John 1:1–3). Of course, He hasn't always been known as Jesus of Nazareth. The Bible tells us that He is God, eternally preexistent before the "incarnation." He is "the image of the invisible God" (Col. 1:15). He created a body for Himself and became a man to suffer and die for the sin of the world.

Consider how the New Testament exalts Jesus of Nazareth. It calls Him "Lord" an incredible 618 times. He is the One to whom all humanity will one day bow the knee. He is called the "Christ" an amazing 543 times, and at times He is referred to as "Christ Jesus." This is because "Christ" ("Messiah," or "anointed one") is a title rather than a name. We do the same thing with our presidents, in using the title "President" before the name of the person in that position.

He is called "Son of Man" 84 times, because He truly was a Man who had the ability to feel pain, experience thirst, and know the torment of fear. He is called "Son of God" 37 times, because He was truly God is human form, manifesting His authority over His creation by walking on water, stilling storms, healing disease, and conquering death.

There has never been anyone like Jesus of Nazareth. Listen to what Philip Schaff said of Him: "This Jesus of Nazareth, without money and arms, conquered more millions than Alexander, Caesar, Mohammed, and Napoleon; without science and learning, He shed more light on things human and divine than all philosophers and scholars combined; without the eloquence of schools, He spoke such words of life as were never spoken before or since, and produced effects which lie beyond the reach of orator or poet; without writing a single line, He set more pens in motion, and furnished themes for more sermons, orations, discussions, learned volumes, works of art, and songs of praise than the whole army of great men of ancient and modern times."]

"Like King Arthur and so many folkloric figures, probably someone who existed, whose teachings and deeds were blown out of proportion by the human imagination. Certainly not the son of God (since I don't think He exists in the first place) or the redeemer of our sins (same deal). Probably a nice guy with some good messages and a lot of prejudices inherent to his time, but little else."

[Not believing in King Arthur will not affect anyone's eternal salvation.]

"Pretty-much like Krishna—there was probably an actual historical figure at some point, who may have even said a few (but probably not all) of the words attributed to him. But what we have today is a hackneyed collection of sayings (with some ancients texts burned as 'heresy' and others canonized). Neither Jesus nor Krishna nor Muhammad nor Joseph Smith left us with any compelling evidence that they had a connection to any God or gods—therefore, while our picture of the historical Jesus is vague and incomplete, we have no reason to particularly much care what he said any more than we care what anyone else says. I liked some of the teachings attributed to Jesus (cast the first stone, do unto others), but some of these ideas (do unto others) already predate Jesus by several centuries anyway. Some of his other teachings I find disagreeable, e.g., I find it appalling that Jesus would advocate that a woman should not get a divorce if she is in an abusive marriage, but only if her husband is adulterous (Matthew 1:31)."

"Jesus, if in fact such a man did ever exist, was just that—a man. He may have had a few radical ideas for his time. He may even have been some sort of magician (as in tricks, not as in supernatural)."

"A relatively enlightened man for his times. Preached simple things such as brotherly love. Likely a real man. Some, like I, think his simple lessons were warped to control the gullible masses (which still works)."

"The carpenter from Bethlehem existed, in all likelihood. He went around giving sermons, but he was not the son of God and he did not speak for God. My father, also an atheist, has speculated that Jesus himself was an atheist and preached his doctrine to give comfort to the minds of people on Earth. I am not sure about this."

[In one such sermon, Jesus gave the ultimate challenge to skeptics: "He who has My commandments and keeps them, it is he who loves Me. And he who loves Me will be loved by My Father, and I will love him and manifest Myself to him" (John 14:21). To find out with 100% absolute certainty that Jesus Christ is God in the flesh, atheists can simply obey His command to repent and believe the gospel, and He will reveal Himself to them. Then they will *know* God exists, because they *know Him*.]

Scriptures

"I think the Bible is simply a book of stories and rules, written by man. It has no divine meaning…It was written to try and explain the unexplainable, but also to control people and make them easier to govern, using the threat of death and hellfire. In a modern society it should not be taken literally at all."

[We are in a modern society (no doubt, every society in history considered itself "modern") and millions take it literally. It is easy to believe that water can be walked on, fish can be multiplied, seas can be opened, storms calmed, etc., when a supernatural nature of God is acknowledged. With God, nothing is impossible.]

"Ha-ha, which Bible? The KJV? NIV? I think the new Oxford annotated Bible is the most derived from the best copies of the earliest Greek manuscripts. It's a lot different from the

KJV and NIV. Not to mention all of the other books that weren't canonized, and other books that have been found since, such as the book of Judas. At any rate, I think it's an excellent resource on the culture of 2,000–3,000 years ago, and with the different changes and additions to the New Testament over the past 2,000 years, an excellent resource on the culture of the past thousand or so years within the Christian churches."

[Atheists will often ask which Bible is right, and point out the fact that there are many versions. The inference is that each one is different, and therefore the Bible has no credibility. So, it's good to agree with them. Explain that there are *thousands* of different versions—there are English versions, Chinese versions, Spanish versions, etc. There are versions in contemporary language, old English, and paraphrases, all written so that sinners of any nation or culture can have access to and understand the Word of God. Then tell them that nowadays we have computer programs that give us the earliest Greek and Hebrew Scriptures, and we can see that they haven't changed down through the ages, as is often claimed.]

"The Bible is a collection of old writings from diverse sources. The authorship of most sections is in question, its historical accuracy is spotty, and it's self-contradictory. I don't trust it any more than I trust other mythologies. Actually, it's not as interesting to read as most other mythologies."

[It's good to ask an atheist how he knows that "its historical accuracy is spotty."]

"Arbitrarily selected religious scribblings writings written by various mortal men from a single culture in the distant past on the other side of the planet. Of large historical interest, due to the significant effects that it has had on history, but having read it, found there is nothing in it to indicate that it was divinely inspired (similarly, the Koran and the Bhagavad-Gita and the Vedas are interesting in their effects on history, but do not contain anything to indicate they were written by anything other than historic, poorly educated, fallible mortal men)."

[Note his "having read it." Many who say that they have read the Bible actually haven't read it through cover to cover. If they maintain that they have, ask them if they know the main *theme* of the Scriptures. When they say that it's a book of rules and moral guidelines, agree with them, but add, "The Old Testament was God's promise to destroy man's greatest enemy—death. The New Testament tells us how He did it."]

"There is no 'official' atheist belief concerning the Bible. My personal opinion is that it is nothing more than a collection of fables which were cobbled together from older pagan fables. The virgin birth, resurrection, great flood, etc., were all borrowed from older religions and given a slightly different spin."

[Again, never hesitate to challenge the atheist's unquestioning faith in history books by asking, "How do you know that to be true?"]

"I think it's just a book of old Judean myths."

"A fine book, certainly, but with little more mystical value than any other mystical book. May have historical value and even some moral lessons here and there, gives insight to civilizations long past. But then, so do the Eddas, the Vedas, the writings of Buddha, or any other mythology."

"Parts of it make a good historical account, but it is a book of myths of varying provenance. Some of the myths would be quite repellent to a modern audience, for example the offering of one's virgin daughters to a crowd of men about to rape runaways in Judges 19:24."

[Many atheists think that because the Scriptures relate the brainless things men did, these are somehow examples of what the believer is to imitate.]

"A book put together by a group of people over a period of time, writing about what they have experienced. Or a fictional book put together, possibly to put people in check."

"It's a work of fiction, very contradictory, and it's not sufficient by itself to prove the existence of anything therein. Not even Jesus."

[What I am about to say goes against the grain of thought held by many respected and wonderful apologists and Bible teachers. I don't see that the mandate of the Church is to convince sinners that the Bible is the Word of God. Rather, I believe that our mandate is to convince sinners that they need a Savior, by preaching the gospel of salvation to them. The early church didn't have the Bible as we know it. There was no such thing as the printing press; besides, few could read. Rather, they heard and believed the gospel. Their salvation wasn't dependent on their belief in the New Testament (which didn't exist yet), but on the fact that they had been regenerated by the Holy Spirit. Christ dwelt within them, and it was with that experience that they went to the mouth of the lion. So, don't feel frustrated when an atheist points to "terrible" judgments of God (and there are many), or what he sees as mistakes in the Bible. Rather, move from his intellect to his conscience by taking him through the Ten Commandments, as Jesus and Paul did with their hearers. Then pray that the Holy Spirit convinces him of sin, righteousness, and judgment to come. Your mandate isn't to intellectually convince him that he should believe the Bible, but that he desperately needs a Savior, so that his faith will not stand on the wisdom of men, but on the power of God.]

"Like other holy books, it was written by people; the books were collected by people. It didn't magically drop from the sky into everyone's homes."

[The irony is that atheists believe that's what happened with everything else in creation.]

"A bit of history mixed with a lot of fiction and distortion. Like every good book, there are important lessons to be learned. However there are some truly disturbing things in it that I would never let my children read."

[This is true. The Scriptures don't hide the sins of mankind. The Bible contains accounts of rape, genocide, cannibalism, suicide, decapitation, incest, terrible violence, adultery, and murder. The most heinous of all is man's rejection of His Creator.]

Heaven and Hell

"I do not believe in either because I don't think there is any valid reason why we would have an afterlife. However, I know some atheists who do believe in an 'afterlife' of sorts, citing that the conscious mind could go on after death. I don't think any atheists believe in Heaven and Hell in the biblical perspective, because it goes against the point about God."

[It is amazing how any seemingly rational human being could think that because he doesn't believe in something, it therefore doesn't exist.]

"I don't believe in Heaven or Hell. When I die, I will push up daisies and feed worms. I strive to make sure people will think fondly of me should I die unexpectedly."

"I assume that you are referring to the Heaven and Hell within Christian dogma, in which case, the modern vision of Hell has little to do with the Bible, but more to do with Dante's divine comedy. Either way, there is no reason to believe that there is any sort of reward or punishment after my life."

"No more plausible than fairies, ghosts, witches, Baba Yaga, etc. I note with interest how Hell doesn't really make an appearance in the Bible until the New Testament—before that the concept is 'Sheol' and has very different connotations. You can ask some practicing Jews about this."

"The carrot and the stick in the chain letter that is the Christian religion."

[Eternal life is not a reward for good works. It is a free gift that comes by grace alone through faith alone. It cannot be earned, and it certainly isn't deserved. This is why the moral Law needs to be used when reasoning with sinners. It puts them before God as devious and guilty criminals, to whom the Judge owes nothing but swift and terrible justice.]

"On par with Atlantis, Narnia, and Middle Earth."

"Non-existent. No reason to even entertain the notion that they exist. Ideas constructed to give people motivation to be 'good' and to not fear death."

"They don't exist. We aren't rewarded or punished after death for anything we do in life."

[An atheist will often ask you where Hell is, and if you can't tell him exactly where it's located, it therefore doesn't exist. So, ask him where the city of Invercargill is located. More than likely he won't know (it's at the bottom of the South Island of New Zealand). Then ask, "So Invercargill doesn't exist, because you can't tell me where it's located? I know Hell exists because I have the greatest authority on this earth—the Word of God."]

"I don't believe God exists. I do not believe in the Bible as the literal inerrant word of God. Thus, Heaven and Hell are, in my opinion, much like God: a feel-good idea that swims in the minds of people, but has little bearing in reality. It's also a nifty way to control people through fear, but I digress. Personally, I think the idea of Hell points to exceptional cruelty. An eternity of pain? That's pure evil. Heaven also sounds pretty boring. I'd rather reincarnate (but alas, I don't believe in that either)."

[The question is often asked, "How could a loving God create Hell?" Think of a how civil judge, who turned a blind eye to murder, would be corrupt and should be brought to justice himself. If the Judge of the Universe is not going to bring murderers to ultimate justice, then He is corrupt. He would be wicked. In the 1990s in the U.S. there were 200,000 murders. Statistics show that during those ten years half of those homicide crimes were unsolved. That means that 100,000 people got away with murder. When we use the Law to show that God is not only loving, but that He is perfect, holy, just, and good, we end up saying, "How can there *not* be a Hell?"]

Sin

"I do not believe there is such a thing as sin, mainly because I do not believe that the Bible is anything other than a load of stories. If there is sin, then there must be moral absolutes, which do not exist because our stance on morality has changed over time. Homosexuality was originally thought of as fine, then the Christians decided it was evil, and now most of us think it is fine again. A continually evolving morality does not have sin, unless the sin were to evolve with it, which makes the entire point of it useless."

[There's a big problem when an atheist denies that sin (evil) exists. All you have to do is ask if murder is wrong, and if he says that it's not, keep on asking if what Hitler did was wrong, or if pedophilia is wrong. You will soon find that he has a moral boundary regarding what is right and what is wrong. God's moral standard is infinitely higher.]

"Sin is the Christian concept that there are certain bad deeds that will send you to Hell. Many of these are antiquated, and part of human nature. Sins are used to scare people into believing that they are going to burn in Hell after they die if they don't ask for forgiveness from a supernatural deity."

"I don't believe in sin. If something is harmful to others, it is wrong regardless of what God thinks about it. If something causes no one else any harm, it is not wrong regardless of what God thinks."

[Is it therefore wrong for a pedophile to secretly take photos of naked children? It's not harmful to the children, since they're not even aware of it.]

"There are such things as right and wrong actions, which are derived from the suffering that is averted or afflicted (see: utilitarianism), along with other factors such as privacy, autonomy, dignity etc. People's actions are right or wrong based on their observed effects in the real world (this one). However, regarding the concept of 'sin,' if 'sin' is defined as disobedience to a given deity, then sin is an entirely pointless concept until we have compelling evidence of the existence—and rightful authority—of that given deity in the first place."

"Against God or man? It is possible to wrong one's fellow man, and such could be called a sin. On the other hand, one can no more sin against God than one can sin against Santa or the Easter Bunny. One cannot sin against that which does not exist."

"Are there are morally wrong things? Yes. Are there things that jeopardize society? Yes. Are they sins, in that they should be punished by forces infinitely vaster than our own and condemn them for an eternity (not a while—an eternity!) of pain? No. There is no crime so terrible to merit that. I can't possibly believe in sin in the religious sense. Some things should be punished for the good of the population and the world as a whole, but for eternity? No."

"I do believe in ethics. These, however, don't come from God but from other people who decide as a group. It's not as solid a basis as God might be, but it's all we can work with. A God not existing, there is nothing that God does not want us to do."

"A human construct used to describe things that our psychology, culture, and evolution–derived 'morals' defines as 'bad.' We all have our own embedded feelings of 'right' or 'wrong.' But these can be subjective. Regardless, there is no such thing as absolute right or wrong. The universe doesn't care."

"I don't believe there are any actions such that will go against my salvation (which I think is what sin means), since I don't think I need to be saved. I do believe there are things that are right and things that are wrong. But they don't coincide with sin. For example, homosexuality, to me, just is, and is just as right or wrong as being blond."

Salvation

"Seeing as I do not believe in an afterlife, the concept of salvation seems ridiculous and unnecessary to me."

"Salvation is a concept in many religions that one can only be 'saved' by following the rules of the particular religion, thereby avoiding 'Hell' and making it in to 'Heaven.'"

"Salvation: From what? I don't need to be saved. You have to prove that I have a soul to save before you can convince me that you have the cure."

"No such thing as 'sin,' or 'Hell,' so no need for salvation. It would be only after we have compelling evidence of a particular God that such a concept is even worth discussing."

"When you die, your consciousness ceases to exist. Salvation is nothing more than wishful thinking."

"There is no such thing as an immortal soul. Everything about who you are—thoughts, emotions, memories, personality—is defined by the chemical and structural makeup of one's brain and physiology. When your brain dies, so does your consciousness and 'self.' Thus, afterlife and concepts such as 'salvation' are meaningless. After life there is only nothing."

"Salvation implies sin, which I don't believe in. I do believe people can change (maybe I am just an optimist, but I do), that people can go past their petty crimes and move on, live better. Some people might not be able, either because of the chemistry in their brains or the conviction of their own righteousness or something else entirely; but many people can change. If that's salvation—and not some feel-good 'God will give you an eternity of pleasure if you just do this'— then I suppose I believe in it. It has nothing to do with God or Jesus or the Bible, and all to do with the human mind and our own capacity to overcome our limitations and grow."

How to Reach an Atheist

To shine the light of the gospel in the hearts of atheists, there are two approaches we could use. We could address their intellect or we could address their conscience.

First, let's look at speaking to the intellect. It's a simple thing to prove the existence of God. To do so, let me quote from *The Evidence Bible* (Bridge-Logos):

When I look at a building, how do I know that there was a builder? I can't see him, hear him, touch, taste, or smell him. Of course, the build*ing* is proof that there was a build*er*. In fact, I couldn't want better evidence that there was a builder than to have the building in front of me. I don't need "faith" to know that there was a builder. All I need is eyes that can see and a brain that works.

Likewise, when I look at a painting, how can I know that there was a painter? Again, the paint*ing* is proof positive that there was a paint*er*. I don't need "faith" to believe in a painter because I can see the clear evidence.

The same principle applies with the existence of God. When I look at creation, how can I *know* that there was a Creator? I can't see Him, hear Him, touch Him, taste Him, or smell Him. How can I know that He exists? Why, creation shows me that there is a Creator. *I couldn't want better proof that a Creator exists than to have the creation in front of me.* I don't need faith to believe in a Creator; all I need is eyes that can see and a brain that works: "For the invisible things of Him *from the creation of the world are clearly seen, being understood by the things that are made,* even His eternal power and Godhead; so that they are without excuse" (Romans 1:20, emphasis added). If, however, I want the builder to *do* something for me, *then* I need to have faith in him. The same applies to God: "Without faith it is impossible to please Him: for He that comes to God must believe that He is, and that He is a rewarder of them that diligently seek Him" (Hebrews 11:6).

As you can see, atheists use numerous arguments to defend their belief systems. So, if you are going to address the intellect (the place of argument), you will find yourself running down a mass of rabbit trails. Instead, do what Jesus did—address the conscience. Consider this analogy.

I'm not big on fishing. I far prefer catching. However, there can be no catching without fishing, so I have made a point of studying the skills that make a difference as to whether I catch or fish.

For example, there are right and wrong ways to bait a hook. Bait should be used to attract fish and at the same time disguise the hook. Fish are not stupid. They aren't going to bite onto a hook that they can see. So, a wise fisherman baits the hook to hide its deadly barbs. Then, when he sees that a fish is nibbling at the bait, he quickly jerks the line and pulls the hook into the jaw, and reels him in.

Apologetics are wonderful bait. I love even the smell of a good apologetical argument. It can't help but attract the fish. He doesn't see anything threatening in an argument about the Bible. He knows he can win any dispute about that book of myths. It has an aroma that attracts him.

God's Law is the hook; and it's that from which he instinctively keeps his distance. It threatens him. That's because it brings the knowledge of sin (see Romans 3:19,20), so his mind is naturally hostile toward the Law. The Scriptures tells us that his carnal mind is at "enmity" with God, and it's "not subject to the law of God, nor indeed can be" (see Romans 8:7). He isn't stupid. If he can see the Law, he's not going to bite. So a wise fisher of men will carefully hide the hook under some good bait.

Jesus did this with the woman at the well. He first spoke of natural water. Nothing threatening here. Then He quickly pulled the hook of the Law into her jaw, by alluding to the

Seventh Commandment to bring the knowledge of sin (see John 4:16).

Paul did a similar thing in Athens. His heart was stirred because the whole city was given over to idolatry (see Acts 17:16). So he baited them by giving an interesting line about their poets, then he quickly jerked the Law into the jaw by preaching against their idolatry (see verses 29,30). They had sinned against God by transgressing the First and Second Commandments; they had "other gods" before Him and therefore needed to repent. The Law brought the Athenians the knowledge of sin.

A Fly on the Rock

Despite these examples in Scripture, many Christians go fishing with powerful and attractive apologetics but leave out the hook. They talk about the existence of God, the infallibility of Scripture, archeological findings, creationism, the fallacy of evolution, the age of the earth, the depth of dust on the moon, etc., but they don't see the necessity of using the Law to bring the knowledge of sin.

Let's be a fly on a rock and listen to a well-equipped apologetical fisher of men. He throws a line toward an unbeliever. There is a nibble, and a conversation begins. Good reason for God's existence is given. Back the sinner comes with an argument for atheism. The Christian quotes Scripture. The atheist retaliates with an argument about "circular reasoning." And there begins an intellectual battle. One says that creation is proof for God's existence and the other says it's the mere product of billions of years of evolution. It's a fascinating conversation—an intellectually challenging match of wits for both parties.

However, the argument has no resolution. It seems to be going on forever and going nowhere. Suddenly, the Christian brings out a powerful point that leaves the atheist with his mouth open. He has no comeback. He is defeated. It's all over. He has lost the argument about the existence of God. Does he then say, "You are right and I am wrong. There is a God and I have sinned against Him. What should I do?" No! Instead he says, "Okay. What about bats? The Bible calls them birds!! Huh? And how about God advocating genocide, and what about slavery? And how about the killing of women who aren't virgins on their wedding night! Your God is nothing but a wicked tyrant!"

There is a very good reason that he isn't giving up the argument. It is because he is thoroughly enjoying the pleasures of sin, and didn't know that life could be so good. Now a religious nut has come along who wants to put an end to all that pleasure. Horrors! He wants him to sit in a boring church, singing old hymns, listening to a deathly boring preacher, and mindlessly clutching a book filled with fairytales. Give up? Are you kidding?

So the unbeliever is going to fight this battle with tooth and nail. He is going to fortify his hedonistic lifestyle with the zeal of a Pharisee, and he will do it with every intellectual argument he can find. And he can easily find websites that give a stack of arguments that promise to justify godlessness. There he can arm himself with a mass of rabbit trails down which he can send the unsuspecting Christian.

Remember, what has gone on between the two of them has been a battle of intellects. Every time a battle is won by the Christian, another skirmish is started. A sinner will use his intellect as a shield to keep the Christian away from his conscience. So if the Christian really wants to win him to the Kingdom of God, he must get to the heart by quickly and purposefully pushing the shield aside and addressing the conscience. He will never give up his darling sins otherwise.

The Scriptures warn, "Each one is tempted when he is drawn away by his own desires and enticed. Then, when desire has conceived, it gives birth to sin; and sin, when it is full-grown, brings forth death" (James 1:15). The sin the unbeliever so loves truly is a "deadly" sin. The lethal poison he drinks is sweet to his taste, but it will take him to Hell. He doesn't believe that because he has no knowledge of sin (see Romans 7:7). Without understanding the consequences of sin, he continues to drink iniquity like water, and he will fight to the death for the right to do so.

Taking Control

Let's say I start a spiritual conversation and have a nibbling fish. He is arguing about bacteria, fossils, Zeus, Thor, and so-called biblical contradictions, and quoting Richard Dawkin's hateful words. As he says God is a monster and Jesus was a liar, I quietly think to myself, "The Jerk." Then, motivated by love, I deliberately take control of the conversation and jerk the Law into his rapidly moving jaw. I am a fisher of men, and I don't want this man to be cast into the lake of fire. I don't want him to be damned in Hell forever. I therefore don't let the fish dictate where we are going.

I ask, "Do you think you are a good person?" He says he knows that he's a good person (see Proverbs 20:6). I ask, "Do you think you have kept the Ten Commandments?" He says he doesn't believe in them. I tell him that I wasn't asking if he believed in them; I'm asking if he has kept them. I say, "Let's go through some of them and see how you will do on Judgment Day." He says he doesn't believe in Judgment Day. So I say, "Let's just suppose that there is one, and see how you will do. Have you ever told a lie? Have you ever stolen something?"

This is what Paul did in Romans 2:21–24. He said, "You, therefore, who teach another, do you not teach yourself? You who preach that a man should not steal, do you steal [Eighth Commandment]? You who say, 'Do not commit adultery,' do you commit adultery [Seventh Commandment]? You who abhor idols [First and Second Commandments], do you rob temples? You who make your boast in the law, do you dishonor God through breaking the law? For 'the name of God is blasphemed among the Gentiles because of you [Third Commandment],' as it is written.'"

This is also what Jesus did in Mark 10:18,19: "Why do you call Me good? No one is good but One, that is, God. You know the commandments: 'Do not commit adultery,' 'Do not murder,' 'Do not steal,' 'Do not bear false witness,'

'Do not defraud,' 'Honor your father and your mother.'" He was using the Law to bring the knowledge of sin.

The only thing that will make a sin-loving sinner give up the battle is the fear of the Lord. Scripture says it is fear that will cause him to depart from evil (see Proverbs 16:6). If he doesn't fear future punishment, he won't depart from sin, and the way to produce the fear of the Lord is to do what Jesus did: point to the Law. It's to do what Paul did: point to the Law. The sinner must be made to tremble (see Acts 24:25). Jerk the hook into the jaw, and do it quickly.

Knowledge that God has appointed a Day in which He will judge the world in righteousness makes sinners see that it's in their best interest to depart from sin. But, if I may say so, we depart somewhat unwillingly. Fleeing from wrath doesn't produce contrition (sorrow for sin). Seeing the cross in all its horror does. Knowing that I am a lawbreaker, and that there are terrible consequences for my actions, makes me fear. But seeing Almighty God pay my fine in the life's blood of His precious Son brings me sorrow. It breaks my hard heart. The Law produces terror. The cross produces contrition. Without the Law that cruel cross has little meaning. The greater I see my sin in the light of God's Law (see Romans 7:13), the greater I will understand and appreciate the mercy shown to me at Calvary's cross.

So, use good apologetics. Fish with the best bait you can find. Then carefully hide the hook, and as soon as the fish nibbles, jerk the line—swing to the Law. Don't wait. Do it quickly. Don't let the sinner shield his conscience for another precious minute. He may not have that long.

My ministry partner, Kirk Cameron, found himself on a plane from Los Angeles to Colorado. Shortly after the flight began, he heard an announcement from the captain saying that the landing gear hadn't retracted correctly, so they were turning back to LAX. The captain soberly told everyone to familiarize themselves with the emergency procedure, and then he asked marshals and military personnel on board to man the emergency exits. This was serious.

Kirk decided that he had better witness to the people sitting next to him. He told them that it was at times like this that it was a good idea to make sure you are right with God. He then took them through the Ten Commandments and shared the good news of the cross.

As they approached the landing, the captain said, "Brace! Brace! Brace!" and the flight attendant kept saying every 60 seconds, "Head down! Head down!" It was extremely traumatic. Kirk said that as they approached the ground, all he could think of was his wife and six children.

Fortunately, the actual landing was without incident. Here's the point. Kirk said that when he spoke to those who sat next to him, he didn't talk to them about the age of the earth or evolution. He knew that there was an extreme urgency for him to address their conscience and talk about the awkward issues of sin, righteousness, and judgment.

Everyone is currently in emergency mode. Death could snatch them into eternity in a heartbeat. So, take courage for their sake, and cut to the chase.

From Atheism to Christ

I was an atheist who was an avid supporter of the Rational Response Squad and Infidel Guy show. I was even going to make my own show at one time to air on Free Thought media (the online programming site that hosted those shows).

Since then, through an unexpected journey, I made my way to the Lord. Though I know many Christians leave to become atheists, there are some of us who also did it the other way around.

Though I was an atheist, I was still a conservative Republican. I witnessed how the Left has tried to shift culture into a point of complacent moral relativism. People were no longer evil; they were misunderstood. There were more excuses than remedies. Along with moral relativism, I noticed that we also had pushed the whole concept of self-accountability out the window.

As silly as it sounds, that was a seed planted in my spirit. I saw that this "manmade" morality had holes in its structure. Logic would tell one that a house, no matter how nice, can't be built on a shifting foundation.

I listened closely to the words you were all saying, even when I was against you. One thing that separated you from all other ministries is that you weren't using emotion and ultra-kindness to entice people. There was a blatant truth. It was like medicine—it might not taste good going down, but the results will amaze. I was also intrigued with the concept that we are indeed evil if we see it through the eyes of perfect justice (which is God's) and not through our shifting justice code.

I know it sounds weird, but it was the fact that there wasn't a lovey-dovey, feel-goody tag to God's justice that made me take this journey. The simplicity of God's justice shot through my heart like a fiery arrow. It hit me that only man can take something simple and make it so complex and gray.

Logic and reason brought me here. I know I don't know everything about God, but I know I don't want to be a liar, a blasphemer, or an adulterer.

There were no tears or emotional outbreak. It was more like a wake-up call that I have to get things in order. Funny, what I once hated about your ministry is the one thing that saved me.

I know I have to do this with baby steps, but I'm glad I'm doing it. I had to lose some atheist friends (and family members) along the way, but I want perfect justice to follow. Thanks for your good work that you do.

— *Brent A.*

Witnessing to an Atheist

You: Hello. How are you doing?

April: Okay.

You: Where are you from?

April: Berkeley.

You: Interesting. My name is [your name here].

April: I'm April.

You: Nice to meet you, April. I have a question for you. What do you think happens after someone dies?

April: Nothing.

You: How do you know that?

April: It's just something I believe.

You: Are you an atheist?

April: Yes, I am.

You: Why are you an atheist?

April: Because there's no proof that God exists.

You: Let me ask you a question. When you look at a building, how do you know that there was a builder?

April: The building exists.

You: Right. When you look at a painting, how can you know that there was a painter?

April: Because the painting exists.

You: Right. The paint*ing* is proof that there was a paint*er*. Paintings don't happen by themselves, and creation is proof that there is a Creator. Think of all the things that surround us—flowers, birds, trees, the sun, the moon, the stars, the seasons. Think of the marvels of the human body—your eyes, for instance. Man has never invented a camera lens anywhere near as intricate as the human eye, with its 137 million light-sensitive cells. Does that make sense?

April: Nope. I don't buy it. You can't relate a painting and a building to creation. There's a big difference between the two. Creation is alive. It came about through evolution over millions of years. There's no proof that God exists. Besides, who made God?

You: He is eternal. He dwells outside the dimension of time —with no beginning or end.

April: No. There's no proof that God exists. You guys are just anti-science and you use religion and the fear of Hell to get simple people to do what you want. Besides, I know an atheist named Dan Parker who was a Christian preacher for 19 years. But he saw the light back in 1984, and became an atheist. How do you answer that?

You: Dan never knew the Lord. He was a false convert, what the Bible calls a "stony-ground" or "thorny-ground" hearer, who fell away from Christianity when temptation exposed him as being a fraud. Judas only lasted three years, but Dan faked it for an amazing 19 years.

[It's vital to understand the principles of true and false conversion when dealing with atheists, as many of them are bitter products of Catholicism, or of the unbiblical methods of modern evangelism. You can freely listen to "True and False Conversion" on www.livingwaters.com.]

[Notice that you have been speaking to April in the realm of her intellect. You've started there to build a relationship with her, and are showing her respect by gracefully letting her give her opinions. Now it's time to swing to her conscience.]

You: April, let's suppose that there is a Heaven, just for a moment. Do you think you are good enough to go there? Are you a good person?

[Because you are just asking her to suppose (imagine) that Heaven exists, she doesn't feel threatened. Besides, she is convinced that she is morally a good person, so there's no threat if she goes along with you.]

April: Of course. I'm a very good person.

You: How many lies do you think you have told, in your whole life? Not "white" lies, but real lies.

[There has been no mention of her moral responsibility to God, so she will have no problem boasting about her sins.]

April: A bundle.

You: *Real* lies?

April: Yeah, real lies.

You: How many? Ten? Hundreds?

April: Hundreds?

You: What do you call someone who tells lies?

April: They are human—everyone lies.

You: Yes. But what would you call *me* if I told lies?

April: A liar.

You: Have you ever stolen anything, in your whole life, even if it was small?

April: Yes. But they were only small things, and it was in the past, when I was younger.

You: What do you call someone who steals things?

April: A thief. I see where you are going with this. You think I'm going to Hell.

You: I didn't say that. Stay with me, April. I know that you don't believe in God, but have you ever used His name in vain?

April: All the time. So what? It's just a word.

You: Let me explain what you are doing. I know you aren't convinced of the fact that God gave you life, but He did. He gave you eyes to see the beauty of this incredible creation, ears to listen to good music, and taste buds to enjoy all the wonderful foods. He lavished His kindness upon you, then you have taken His holy name and used it as a cuss word to express disgust. That's a very serious crime in His eyes—it's called "blasphemy."

April: I don't buy it.

You: That doesn't matter. One to go. Jesus said that whoever looks with lust has already committed adultery in the heart. Have you ever lusted?

April: Plenty of times.

You: So, April, here's a summation of what we have found about you. You are not a good person at all. You've admitted that (and I'm not judging you) you are a liar, a thief, a blasphemer, and an adulterer at heart; and you have to face God on Judgment Day whether you believe in Him or not. You were right about going to Hell. The Bible says that all liars will have their part in the lake of fire, and that no thief, blasphemer, or adulterer will enter Heaven.

April: I don't believe Hell exists.

You: Would you bet your life on it?

April: Yep.

You: Well, you are. If I stood in front of a judge and said, "Judge, I know that I am guilty of murder, but I don't believe in the electric chair," it's not going to change anything. My unbelief doesn't change reality. So, does it concern you that if you died right now and God gave you justice, you would end up in Hell forever?

April: Not much.

You: Have you ever been in a dentist's chair when he hits a raw nerve in your tooth?

April: Yes.

You: Did you like it?

April: No.

You: Imagine what Hell will be like. It is a place of terrible, unending pain and torment. April, it's got to concern you. You love life, don't you?

April: Of course I do.

You: Do you know what God did for us, so that we could avoid Hell?

April: No. What did He do?

You: He became a morally perfect human being—Jesus of Nazareth—and gave His life as a sacrifice for the sin of the world. We broke God's Law (the Ten Commandments) but because Jesus paid our fine on the cross 2,000 years ago, God can dismiss our case. He can commute our death sentence. The Bible says, "God demonstrates His own love toward us, in that while we were still sinners, Christ died for us." God proved His great love for you through the cross. Then Jesus rose from the dead, and defeated the power of the grave. April, if you repent and trust the Savior, God will forgive your sins and grant you everlasting life. Does that make sense?

[You are not preaching about "intelligent design" to an atheist. You are preaching about an Intelligent Designer: "For we do not preach ourselves, but Christ Jesus the Lord, and ourselves your bondservants for Jesus' sake" (2 Corinthians 4:5).]

April: Yes, it does.

You: So where would you go, according to the Bible, if you died right now?

April: I would probably go to Hell.

You: What are you going to do about it?

April: I will think about what you have said.

You: Please do that. There's nothing more important than where you will spend eternity. Thanks for listening. May I give you a Bible?

April: Okay, but I may not read it.

If you are praying for any atheists, this testimony should encourage you to never give up on anyone!

I was a true atheist, addicted to pornography and a big fan of torture. I hated the Bible and literally looked at 'contract killer' as a career option. I favored abortion of potentially disabled children and agreed with the majority of Adolf Hitler's statements about the disabled and invalid. I fantasized about murder and contemplated suicide and held nothing but hatred in my heart for anyone who told me I was wrong. In short, I was the most degenerate scum to ever walk the Earth. That God saved me is still so far beyond my comprehension I have to wake up every day and think "wow."

Nowadays, I work at the church I once hated going to. I greet daily a pastor I once did everything in my power to ignore, and I serve as an assistant to a youth leader I once despised. I play in the Sunday band and teach drums to young boys of the congregation for extra income. I teach Sunday school and am a regular fixture at the weekly prayer meetings and church events. People who have known me throughout the process have told me how astonishing it is to have seen the transformation. But no one is as impressed as me with how God has changed my heart and my life.

So, that's me. I'm a 6'6", 19-year-old motorcyclist who plays drums, carries a Bible, vacuums a church, writes scripts that will never be made films, and carries around a hefty supply of Way of the Master Radio on his iPod.

—*Jacques R.*

My Testimony (in a nutshell)...

Wendy Branam

For many years I longed for peace
And something that would bring relief
From all the sorrow, guilt and shame
Resulting from mistakes I'd made.

Time and time again I prayed
Jesus, come into my heart today
Each time I thought I had figured it out
But a short time later returned the doubt.

Then one day on the radio
I heard a different kind of show
The Way of the Master was the name
Law then grace they did proclaim.

Each day I listened so I could hear more
Then came conviction too strong to ignore
I wrote and asked for help one day
The response: We'll gladly show you the way.

In the mirror of God's law
The magnitude of my sin I saw
Like a light the Law did shine
On all the sin I'd tried hide.

With my conscience having done its part
By making ready for grace my heart
I understood that I needed to be saved
From the wrath of God on Judgment Day.

The good news of the gospel now made sense
I could be pardoned at Christ's expense
Jesus bore God's wrath for me
When He bled and died on Calvary.

Humbled, on my knees I bowed
And asked God to save me now
For all my sin I said, "I'm sorry"
And promised to live for His honor and glory.

With a contrite heart, I did pray
From these sins I'll turn away
I put my faith and trust in Christ
And at that moment received new life.

MODERN CHRISTIANITY

Perhaps one of the largest groups of unsaved "religious" people in the world are those who sit in the pews of our churches. Those referred to as false converts are not what are often called "traditional churchgoers" ("Christmas and Easter Christians") or "nominal Christians." Rather, these are people who profess to be born again, but have never found a place of biblical repentance. They don't have "the things that accompany salvation." There's no fruit in their lives to say that they have been regenerated by the Holy Spirit. They sit *among* the Church but they are not *part* of the Church.

Bill Bright, founder of Campus Crusade for Christ, wrote, "Here in the United States, one-third of all adults identify themselves as born-again, evangelical Christians. More than 100 million attend church each Sunday and more millions listen to Christian radio and television programs regularly. But we have a serious problem. These facts are not reflected in the life of our nation. According to our surveys, fewer than 50 percent of the church members in America are sure of their salvation...and a bare 2 percent regularly share their faith in Christ. Obviously something is tragically wrong."[32]

Background

Something certainly *is* tragically wrong, and it has been wrong for the last 100 or so years.[33] The contemporary Church has forsaken biblical evangelism. Modern Christianity has failed to use God's Law to bring the knowledge of sin, and has therefore filled the Church with false converts.[34] These false converts have named the name of Christ, but have never departed from iniquity ("lawlessness"—transgression of the Ten Commandments).

It is a neglect of the Law that has resulted in our churches being filled with tares among the wheat, foolish virgins among the wise, bad fish among the good, and goats among the sheep. This is why so many profess Christ and have no assurance of salvation. They have no assurance *because they are not saved*. This is why so many profess to have the love of God in their hearts, and at the same time couldn't care less that the world is going to Hell. *Every* Christian should be horrified beyond words that any human being could be cast into Hell. Such thoughts should take us from our knees and drive us to reach into this dark world with the light of the glorious gospel. If it doesn't, something is radically wrong. Listen to Charles Spurgeon, the Prince of Preachers: "Someone asked, 'Will the heathen who have never heard the gospel be saved?' It is more a question with me whether we—who have the gospel and fail to give it to those who have not—can be saved."

So it's very common to meet people who are products of the modern gospel—they say that they are Christians, and yet you find yourself suspecting that something isn't quite right. Let's look at their beliefs about God, Jesus, the Scriptures, Heaven and Hell, and see why they believe as they do.

Who Is God?

Idolatry is the fertile soil from which a false profession grows. Any sinner who truly captures a glimpse of God's true character, will (like Isaiah) fall on his face in true repentance (Isaiah 6:1–8). The Scriptures tell us that "by the fear of the Lord men depart from evil" (Proverbs 16:6). So few fear God because so few pulpits preach the fear of God. Rarely do sinners hear that God is angry with the wicked every day,[35] that if they are friends with this world they are enemies of God,[36] and that His wrath abides on them.[37] Every time they sin, they are storing up His wrath that will come upon them on the Day of Wrath.[38]

Rather, they hear the unbiblical gospel of "God has a wonderful plan for your life" or simply that God wants them to prosper. Instead of being told to repent because they have offended a holy God, they are told that God will solve their problems and fill their God-shaped vacuum.

So instead of the prodigal leaving the pigsty of his sins, and returning to his father in repentance because he has sinned against him, he returns because he has run out of money and he is hungry. The motive for responding to the "wonderful plan" gospel is that he has issues and problems, and he wants God to be his divine butler. In his lukewarm state, he looks upon God not as his Lord, but as his servant —as one who will come running at his beck and call when He is needed.

There is no fear of God before his eyes because the fear of God has not been put before his eyes. What Bill Bright saw in his survey was the tragic result of another gospel that produced another harvest.

Who Is Jesus?

Think of a rebellious youth who gets drunk and drives through a small town at a dangerous speed of 65 mph.[39] As everything in the town was horse-drawn, they had no law against speeding. The speedster therefore hadn't broken the law because there wasn't one.

The town counsel gathered and passed a law stating that 30 mph was the maximum speed. A massive fine would be imposed on anyone who violated the law and endangered lives.

The drunken speedster came through again, this time at 75 mph. When he was stopped, he had no concern about what he was doing wrong because he knew nothing about the law. It was only when the law was read to him that he understood that he was in big trouble. It was its threat of punishment that sobered him. He had no money and no words of defense, so he was thrown into prison.

As he sat in hopeless despair, his father came to the prison door and explained that he had paid the fine in full. The youth was free to go. The man had sold all his worldly goods to pay his son's fine. Knowledge of his father's sacrifice left the son broken, and wanting nothing more than to live a life that was pleasing to his father.

To the false convert, the Savior is the One who died for his sins. He paid his fine. However, you will find that there is a shallow understanding of the sacrifice of the Father. This is because he has no knowledge of God's Law. It's only when he sees his terrible sin (that he is a terrible Law-breaker) and that he deserves consequent damnation, that he will understand the unspeakable sacrifice that the Father made in Jesus of Nazareth. The Law makes grace abound. It makes make Jesus precious to him.[40]

Scriptures

A false convert may believe that the Scriptures are God's Word, but he usually doesn't see them as his life's sustenance. He doesn't *desire* the sincere milk of the Word that he may grow, because he hasn't tasted of the goodness of the Lord. The saying is true: "This Book will keep you from sin, or sin will keep you from this Book." Because he doesn't soak himself in the Word, he is ignorant about subjects such as the holiness of God, the Law of God and its true function, and the reality of true and false conversion.

Heaven and Hell

A false convert usually lacks any depth of sound doctrine. He couldn't explain the basics of how we are justified or sanctified. He may say that Jesus is the only way to God, and yet with a little probing you will find that he usually ascribes to a form of universalism. This is because, without the Law, God seems unjust to condemn sinners (most of whom he sees as reasonably good people) to eternity in Hell. More than likely he will believe that everyone goes to Heaven, except people like Adolf Hitler. Hell is a place for those *he* thinks are worthy of punishment.

Sin and Salvation

A false convert thinks lightly of sin. This is why he believes he can be a Christian and still have sin in his life.[41] He is like the pig that wallows in the mire. Pigs wallow to cool their flesh, and because the false convert hasn't repented, his flesh needs to be continually cooled through sin. He is truly a "worker of iniquity" (see Matthew 7:23) who sees nothing wrong with fibs, not keeping his word, taking (small) things that belong to other people, and giving himself to sexual lust.[42] His reasoning is, "Who doesn't do that?" and "God understands." He has his weaknesses. You may even hear blasphemy slip from his lips.

The false convert has often been through the motions of modern "conversion" (responded to an altar call, prayed a "sinner's prayer," etc.), and has consequently been given assurance by the preacher that he is saved.

How to Reach a False Convert

It's important to keep in mind that a spurious convert may say all the right things. He may say that he loves the Lord.

He may be in fellowship, and even have regular time of prayer. What then can we say to these people to awaken them to their terrible condition? I have found that there are two questions that will help to expose his true state. The first is to ask him when was the last time he read his Bible. The second (and more revealing) question is, does he think that he's a good person?

Use the moral Law (like a mirror) to show him his true state before a holy God. However, once you have shown the seriousness of sin, explain that seeing sin in its true light has been what has been lacking in his life. This will help him understand why he has never truly repented. Why should he repent if his sin isn't too bad? Ignorance of the Law has left him seeing himself as a basically good person. Without the light of the Law, he has never seen the character of a holy God, known the fear of God, or understood the sacrifice of the cross.

Think of yourself as a good doctor. His patient is sure that he is healthy, but the doctor sees a number of serious symptoms on his flesh that alarm him. So he merely keeps asking questions of his patient, until the patient too is concerned for his own well-being.

Be bold and very thorough in your examination. You can do this if you are motivated by love and concern. Make sure both of those virtues are very evident in your tone.

Witnessing to a False Convert

You: Hi, how are you doing?

Eric: Good.

You: Are you from around here?

Eric: Yes.

You: I'm Ray. What's your name?

Eric: Eric.

You: Eric, I have a question for you. What do you think happens after someone dies? Do you think that they are reincarnated, or do you think that there's a Heaven?

Eric: I think that there's Heaven and a Hell.

You: Who goes to Heaven?

Eric: All who believe in Jesus Christ.

You: Are you a Christian?

Eric: Yes, I am.

You: Have you been born again?

Eric: Yes. Definitely.

You: Tell me about it. What happened?

Eric: I used to have a pretty bad drug and alcohol problem, and when I asked Jesus into my life, it completely went away. Praise the Lord.

You: Great. Eric, when did you last read your Bible?

Eric: I don't know. A while ago.

You: How long ago?

Eric: A couple of months.

You: Do you think that you are a good person?

Eric: Yes. I know that I'm a sinner, but I am basically a good person.

You: So you wouldn't say that your heart is deceitfully wicked?[43]

Eric: No, definitely not. My heart is good.[44]

You: I'm a little concerned for you, Eric. Here's why. In Mark 10:18 Jesus said that there is none good but God. So, who is right, you or Jesus? Couple that with the fact that you haven't been reading your Bible, and it makes me think that something is wrong. There's nothing more important than your eternal salvation. We are talking about where you will spend eternity. Let's use a car as an analogy. Is God is the driver's seat, passenger seat, back seat, or in the trunk?

Eric: The passenger seat.

You: He should be in the driver's seat, if He is your Lord. Do you remember what it says in Matthew 7:21–23? "Not everyone who says to Me, 'Lord, Lord,' shall enter the kingdom of heaven, but he who does the will of My Father in heaven. Many will say to Me in that day, 'Lord, Lord, have we not prophesied in Your name, cast out demons in Your name, and done many wonders in Your name?' And then I will declare to them, 'I never knew you; depart from Me, you who practice lawlessness!'" Imagine that happening to you.

Eric: I hear what you are saying.

You: Eric, I want to do something that will really help you get this issue cleared up once and for all. This will help you. You said that you are a good person. Let's find out if that's true by looking for a few moments at the Ten Commandments. Okay?

Eric: Okay.

[Then you take Eric through the Ten Commandments—opening up their spiritual nature, as you would anyone else. Once he sees himself in the mirror of God's Law, it will send him to the cleansing water of the gospel.]

From False Conversion to Christ

I "accepted Jesus" in 1977 after praying a "sinner's prayer" from a Christian book in my office. I visited many churches but everywhere I visited I found a very lukewarm church. I ended up believing the faith message. I went to a local Bible college and became a licensed and ordained minister of the gospel "WOF [Word of Faith] style." Soon afterwards I became the administrator of a WOF church with about a thousand members.

After that I pastored a small church for about two years. I started watching "The Way of the Master" in 2005 on TBN and thought it was great, but did not fully grasp the underlying message. In March 2006 I went to a faith church website to watch one of my favorite faith teachers. To my surprise I noticed that Ray Comfort had taught at their conference. I decided to watch the two messages that Ray taught. The first was "Hell's Best Kept Secret."[45] This message raised my eyebrow and my curiosity. I knew it was scripturally correct and wondered why I had never heard this kind of message before. The next night I watched "True and False Conversion." As I listened to Ray describe, plainly and scripturally, what a Christian was and was not, I fell under conviction for my sin. I was under a powerful conviction for three days crying out to God in repentance and begging for God to save me. I trembled before Him, realizing that I believed I was saved, but after examining myself scripturally, I knew I was LOST! How could I be deceived for 27 years? I had read the Bible many, many times, studied it, meditated on it, loved it and preached it. I was horrified!

Today, because of the faithful preaching of the Word of

God and by God's grace, I am truly changed. My life has been radically different. I am very sensitive to sin and now the fruit of God's Spirit is growing in me. I have taught The Way of the Master class[46] at my church and regularly share my faith. I am also of the reformed faith now. My family has been dramatically changed with many coming to true faith in Christ. I am very thankful to Ray for being obedient to God and thankful to God for redeeming me out of my deception.

Please continue to be kind, patient, and understanding to those who do not understand the gospel—people like me. A. W. Tozer and Leonard Ravenhill both were bemoaning the fact that the church in America was almost lost in the '60s. When I came to church in the late '70s I wanted to know God and all I found was falsehood. When I was a teenager I went to a Baptist church and was asked to leave by the other youth because I didn't fit in their "clique." I left; no one cared. When I "accepted Jesus" in 1977, I went to Lutheran, Methodist, and Pentecostal churches and finally stayed at a Baptist church. I again was unwelcome and found no one serious about reading and living the Scriptures. I heard the faith message on the radio and thought, at last someone who loves the Bible and is willing to believe it. I had no understanding to properly interpret the Bible and after a while trusted these teachers. There are many people in all these doctrinally wrong churches—in "Word of Faith" churches—who sincerely want to know God and unknowingly went into a place called church and were led astray. Please continue what you do and continue to reach out to help all who are false converts.

—Al H.

NOTES

1. www.harrisinteractive.com/harris_poll/index.asp?PID=707.

2. The witnessing encounters in this book are based on the author's personal witnessing experiences with thousands of people from many different faiths. While these conversations are composites, the actual questions and objections that are raised are true to life.

3. www.watchtower.org/library/jt/index.htm?article=article_01.htm.

4. *The Watchtower*, Oct. 1, 1967, p. 587.

5. www.johnankerberg.org/Articles/apologetics/AP0100W4.htm.

6. www.apologeticsindex.org/j02ab.html#resources.

7. *Let God Be True*, p. 9 <www.greatcom.org/resources/handbook_of_todays_religions/01chap05/default.htm>.

8. www.cnview.com/on_line_resources/facts_you_should_know_about_jehovahs_witnesses.htm.

9. *Watchtower*, December 15, 1989, p. 30.

10. *Keep Watch Over Yourselves...*, p. 35.

11. www.rapidnet.com/~jbeard/bdm/Cults/jw.htm.

12. www.towerwatch.com/Witnesses/Beliefs/their_beliefs.htm.

13. www.johnankerberg.org/Articles/apologetics/AP0100W4.htm.

14. Copyright Answering Islam, originally published at www.answering-islam.org/Testimonies/yucel.html. Printed with permission.

15. www.vatican.va/archive/catechism/p3s1c3a3.htm#ten.

16. www.catholic.org/bible/ten_commandments.php.

17. www.vatican.va/archive/catechism/p123a12.htm#III (#1033-1037).

18. www.vatican.va/archive/catechism/p123a12.htm#III (#1031).

19. www.gotquestions.org/plenary-indulgences.html.

20. www.scborromeo.org/ccc/p2s2c1a3.htm.

21. The Catechism of the Catholic Church, p. 707 (#2683).

22. For a few examples, see Acts 9:13; 9:32; 9:41; 26:10; Romans 8:27; 12:13; 15:25,26; 15:31; 16:2; 16:15; 1 Corinthians 6:1; 2 Corinthians 1:1; Ephesians 1:1; 4:11,12.

23. www.vatican.va/archive/ccc_css/archive/catechism/p2s2c2a4.htm.

24. Tan Swee Eng, "A Basic Buddhism Guide." www.Buddhanet.net, 2004, emphasis added.

25. www.religionfacts.com/buddhism/beliefs.htm.

26. www.christianitytoday.com/ct/2001/june11/15.64.html.

27. www.buddhist-temples.com/buddhism-facts/buddhist-belief.html.

28. www.buddhist-temples.com/buddhism-facts/buddhism-for-beginner.html.

29. www.raycomfortfood.blogspot.com.

30. In their responses, atheists were required to capitalize "God" and "Jesus," something they normally don't do.

31. Leader of small community near Travesser Park, New Mexico. Travesser claims that in March 2000 God told him, "You are Messiah," and he has since asserted, "I am the embodiment of God. I am divinity and humanity combined" (May 1 & 4, 2008, Associated Press).

32. www.10basicsteps.com/english/personalword.htm.

33. See *The Way of the Master* (Bridge-Logos).

34. Please take the time to listen to "Hell's Best Kept Secret" and "True and False Conversion" on www.LivingWaters.com.

35. See Psalm 7:11.

36. See James 4:4.

37. See John 3:36.

38. See Romans 2:5–9.

39. This story is adapted from *Hell's Best Kept Secret* (Whitaker).

40. See 1 Cor. 16:22; 1 Peter 1:7,8.

41. A true convert may sin, but it is not willful. If he says that he loves God and yet plans to sin, something is radically wrong. A true con-

vert *falls*, rather than *dives* into sin.

42. A poll conducted by a Christian website indicates that 50% of all Christian men and 20% of all Christian women are addicted to pornography, and the problem is escalating in both men and women who regularly attend church (www.worldmag.com/articles/10555).

43. See Jeremiah 17:9.

44. See Proverbs 20:6.

45. Available on www.livingwaters.com.

46. The Basic Training Course, available through www.livingwaters.com.

RESOURCES

Please visit our website and sign up for our free weekly e-mail update. To learn to share your faith the way Jesus did, don't miss these helpful resources:

- "Hell's Best Kept Secret" and "True & False Conversion" audio messages (listen freely online)
- *The Way of the Master* (our most important book)
- *Hell's Best Kept Secret*
- *How to Bring Your Children to Christ…& Keep Them There*
- *How to Know God Exists*
- *God Doesn't Believe in Atheists*
- The Way of the Master Radio (www.WayoftheMasterRadio.com)
- "The Way of the Master" television program (www.WayoftheMaster.com)
- "Transformed" and "Deeper" conferences

For Ray Comfort's resources, online Bible School, and training Academy, visit **www.livingwaters.com**, call 800-437-1893, or write to: Living Waters Publications, P.O. Box 1172, Bellflower, CA 90706.

The Evidence Bible

"*The Evidence Bible* is specially designed to reinforce the faith of our times by offering hard evidence and scientific proof for the thinking mind."

—DR. D. JAMES KENNEDY

The Evidence Bible, based on more than two decades of research, has been commended by Josh McDowell, Franklin Graham, Dr. Woodrow Kroll, and many other Christian leaders.

- Learn how to show the absurdity of evolution.

- See from Scripture how to prove God's existence without the use of faith.

- Discover how to prove the authenticity of the Bible through prophecy.

- See how the Bible is full of eye-opening scientific and medical facts.

- Read fascinating quotes from Darwin, Einstein, Newton, and other well-known scientists.

- Learn how to share your faith with your family, neighbors, and coworkers, as well as Muslims, Mormons, Jehovah's Witnesses, etc.

- Glean evangelistic wisdom from Charles Spurgeon, John Wesley, George Whitefield, D. L. Moody, John MacArthur, and many others.

- Discover answers to 100 common objections to Christianity.

School of Biblical Evangelism

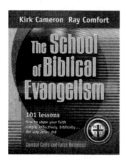

Do you want to deepen your passion for the lost, for the cross, and for God? Then look no further. Join more than 10,000 students from around the world in the School of Biblical Evangelism, to learn how to witness and defend the faith.

With 101 lessons on subjects ranging from basic Christian doctrines to knowing our enemy, from false conversions to proving the deity of Jesus, you will be well-equipped to answer questions as you witness to anyone. This study course will help you to prove the authenticity of the Bible, provide ample evidence for creation, refute the claims of evolution, understand the beliefs of those in cults and other religions, and know how to reach both friends and strangers with the gospel.

"A phenomenal course."
—Jim Culver

"Awesome… This course should be required in every theological seminary."
—Spencer S. Hanley

"As a graduate of every other evangelism course I can find, yours by far has been the best."
—Bill Lawson

Join online at **www.biblicalevangelism.com**
or, to obtain the entire course in book form,
call **800-437-1893** or visit fine bookstores everywhere